BLOODY BRITISH HISTORY

CAMDEN

DICK WEINDLING
& MARIANNE COLLOMS

The
History
Press

First published in 2013

The History Press
The Mill, Brimscombe Port
Stroud, Gloucestershire, GL5 2QG
www.thehistorypress.co.uk

British Library Cataloguing in Publication Data.
A catalogue record for this book is available from the British Library.

ISBN 978 0 7524 8738 0

Typesetting and origination by The History Press
Printed in Great Britain

CONTENTS

INTRODUCTION

CAMDEN WAS FORMED by amalgamating the three boroughs of Hampstead, St Pancras and Holborn in 1965, when London's local government was restructured and larger administrative areas created. Today's Camden extends from Highgate and Hampstead, in the north, and south through Kilburn, Camden and Kentish Towns to Bloomsbury and Holborn – and reaching almost as far as the River Thames.

This book contains bloody and bizarre events that occurred over a 2,000-year time span: Roman attacks, grave robbing, duels and highwaymen all feature, as do two of the twentieth-century's best-known crimes – the cases of Dr Crippen and Ruth Ellis. We end with a look at the damage in Camden inflicted by two world wars, with personal stories from eyewitnesses.

Unless otherwise credited, all images are in the collection of the publisher or the authors.

AD 304

EARLY CAMDEN HISTORY

IT MAY COME as something of a surprise to find that a brutal act in Rome AD 304 affected the history of Camden. That year, an orphan boy from Phrygia (a part of modern Turkey) was martyred by the Emperor Diocletian for his Christian faith. Pancratius was just fourteen years old when he died; he was later beatified as St Pancras. He was popular with early Christians, and St Pancras parish took its name from the church in Pancras Road, a very old establishment that may date from the fourth century.

In 1965 the three boroughs of St Pancras, Hampstead and Holborn were amalgamated to create Camden. A pillar of Gloucester Gate Bridge, Regent's Park, has a replica bronze plaque depicting his martyrdom: the original was stolen when repairs were carried out in 2002. Here, Pancratius is shown being attacked by a fierce animal, though other reports say he was beheaded.

Soon after the Romans landed, in AD 43, they built Watling Street by straightening out and paving an ancient trackway which linked Kent and St Albans. The road still forms the western boundary of the borough of Camden, today renamed Maida Vale, Kilburn High Road and Shoot-Up Hill. It was extremely dangerous to travel through the dense Middlesex forest that fringed the road, and travellers would

The St Pancras plaque.

gather at Kilburn Priory to make the journey in groups. The priory was formed in about 1130 when a hermit called Godwyn gave his cell to the Abbot of Westminster, who, with the agreement of the Bishop of London, established a small group of nuns at Kilburn. Although it struggled financially, the priory continued to support travellers for 400 years. Then, in 1536, it was dissolved as a lesser monastery (under £200 value) by Henry VIII. The 'Nonnerie of Kilnborne' was then only valued at £74 7s 11d, including the priory, farm outbuildings and 46 acres of land. Extensive research has shown that the site was near where today's Priory Road and Belsize Road meet.

There are several myths concerning Roman Camden and Queen Boudica. The first Roman settlement of Londinium lay north of the river, but it was outside the bounds of Camden. In AD 61, barely a decade after it was founded, Londinium lay in ruins, burnt to the ground by the Queen and her Iceni warriors. The Roman invaders had allowed the Iceni to keep their East-Anglian kingdom, but they annexed the territory when Boudica's husband died. Boudica was flogged, and her daughters raped. She led a rebellion against the Romans, first sacking Colchester before moving on to London, and then St Albans. Boudica's army took no prisoners, slaughtering all who opposed them. Various sources say between 70,000 and 80,000 people died. Those who were taken captive by the Britons were subjected to every known form of outrage. The worst and most bestial atrocity committed by their captors was the following: they hung up naked the noblest and

Boudica and her daughters, now immortalised as a statue by the Thames.

most distinguished of the women and then cut off their breasts and sewed them to their mouths, in order to make the victims appear to be eating them; afterwards, they impaled the women on sharp skewers run lengthwise through the entire body. All this they did to the accompaniment of sacrifices, banquets, and other wanton behaviour.

The location of Boudica's final defeat and burial place are unknown. The battle is generally believed to have been fought in the West Midlands, somewhere along Watling Street. There's no evidence it happened in Camden, but the story still persists that the encounter took place at 'Battle Bridge', the old name for the neighbourhood of King's Cross, and that Boudica herself lies buried beneath the station. It even appeared on a panel of historic information used to decorate the hoarding around the station during its recent redevelopment. Excavations have also proved an alternative claim – that Boudica is buried in a tumulus on Hampstead Heath – to be false. The mound is now generally believed to be an artificial feature created to give interest to the landscape.

In 1892 five items of buried treasure were discovered close to the site. Three-year-old Edward Barrington Haynes was with his mother, 'amusing himself in digging up mole-heaps in the neighbourhood of a supposed ancient tumulus', when she saw something gleaming and pulled out what she thought was an old candlestick. Edward then dug up the remaining silver-gilt items. They were initially thought to be worth around £1,000, but sadly the treasure's value soon fell: the British Museum declared that £12 to £13 was closer to the mark. None of the items were buried deeper than 8in beneath the soil. Two square bottles with a Paris hallmark of around 1672 were found, probably for spirits or perfume; a small, flat, two-handled cup was judged to be English and of roughly the same date; and, lastly, two broken items which once formed part of a candelabra or wall sconce were uncovered. As no owner could be traced, the artefacts were ruled to be treasure trove. They were bought by the V&A Museum and put on display later that year.

Although the theory has been widely dismissed, the jury is still out when it comes to Caesar's camp, known as the Brill, near St Pancras Old Church. This was identified by eighteenth-century archaeologist Dr Stukeley, who was not the most reliable historian in later years. He made a detailed sketch of what he thought were the remains of the camp, some still visible on the ground. There were certainly earthworks and, although no link to the Romans has been established, there remains the outside possibility that a camp did exist.

AD 1417

THE CRUEL DEATH OF SIR JOHN OLDCASTLE

ON 14 DECEMBER 1417 crowds gathered to watch a brutal execution on the gallows at the southern end of Tottenham Court Road, close to the gates of the lepers' hospital.

The man sentenced to die was Sir John Oldcastle, a leader of the Lollards, a religious sect that emphasised personal faith and believed everyone should have access to a Bible written in English. At the time Bibles were in Latin and the interpretation of the text was the sole preserve of the established Church.

Oldcastle was a fine soldier, and a trusted supporter of the Prince of Wales, later Henry V. But when Oldcastle stood firm in his religious beliefs he was tried, and convicted, as a heretic. Henry hoped Oldcastle might recant and imprisoned him in the Tower of London for forty days. Instead, Oldcastle escaped, with the help of William Fisher, a parchment maker. William made a fatal mistake by hiding Oldcastle in his home and was hanged, drawn and quartered for his hospitality. It was alleged that Sir John had been plotting to murder the King as he was celebrating Christmas at Eltham Palace. Further rumours claimed that 20,000

of his followers were expected to gather in St Giles's Fields. In the event, however, less than 100 supporters gathered. They were easily captured or dispersed. On 13 February 1414 thirty-eight men were dragged on hurdles from Newgate Prison to St Giles's Fields and hanged, in batches, on four new gallows. Seven were afterwards burned.

A price was put on Oldcastle's head, but he evaded the King's men until

The burning of Sir John Oldcastle.

November 1417, when he was captured in Wales. Brought to London, he was condemned for insurrection and heresy and received a dreadful sentence: to be hanged up by the waist on a chain and burnt alive.

John Foxe's *Actes and Monuments of* describes Oldcastle's last moments:

> And, upon the day anointed, he was brought out of the Tower with his arms bound behind him, having a very cheerful countenance. Then he was laid upon a hurdle ... and so drawn forth to St-Giles-in-the-Fields, where they had set up a new pair of gallows. As he was approaching the place of execution, and was taken from the hurdle, he fell down devoutly upon his knees, desiring Almighty God to forgive his enemies ... Then he was hanged up there by the middle, in chains of iron, and so consumed alive in the fire...

Oldcastle appears as a named friend of Prince Hal in a play used by Shakespeare when writing *Henry IV*. Sources also claim that he was the inspiration for Falstaff.

AD 1665

BRING OUT YOUR DEAD

A Leper Hospital and Plague in Camden

IN THE TWELFTH CENTURY Queen Matilda, the wife of Henry I, ordered that a leper hospital be established in Holborn fields, some distance from the built-up area of London. She provided sixty shillings a year to support fourteen inmates while other citizens also made generous donations. The hospital and its chapel (under royal protection) were dedicated to St Giles, the patron saint of cripples and outcasts. It was one of only three such institutions in England. The walls enclosed grounds that covered the area between the present St Giles High Street, Charing Cross Road and Shaftesbury Avenue.

In 1299 the hospital became a cell of the order of St Lazarus of Jerusalem. The officials protested when Lazarus friars or aged retainers of the Crown were sent to live at St Giles, arguing that healthy people should on no account mix with the diseased. Continued quarrels and poor management meant the hospital was often in debt, and the number of lepers it could support was reduced.

In around 1400, a gallows was set up at the southern end of Tottenham Court Road and it became customary for the condemned man to be given 'the St Giles' bowl' of ale as he passed the hospital gates. As London grew and the

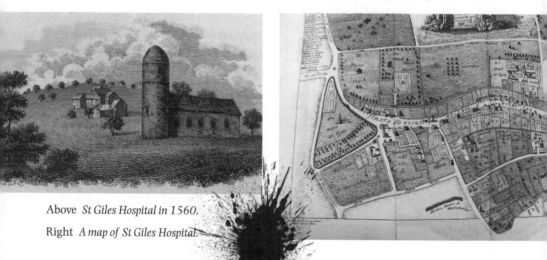

Above *St Giles Hospital in 1560.*

Right *A map of St Giles Hospital.*

gallows moved west to Tyburn, the drink continued to be supplied by a nearby tavern. Jack Sheppard, the notorious highwayman, is said to have returned the bowl part full, saying, 'give the rest to Jonathan Wild', a reference to the double-dealing thief-taker who had turned him in. The hospital closed in 1539 and a new St Giles' church was built on the site of its chapel.

Many outbreaks of plague have been recorded in London. In 1603, a blighted year, some 30,000 citizens died. Many fled the town in terror, but took the disease with them. They crept into yards and outhouses, or died 'under hedges in the fields whereof we have experience weekly here at Hampstead.' During the 1631 epidemic an official visited Highgate twice a week to make certain anyone infected was 'shut up and sequestered from going abroad'.

The Great Plague struck in 1665 and killed 69,000 Londoners. It spread from the poorer streets in and around the church of St Giles, with the first deaths at the northern end of Drury Lane. Rats carried the fleas that spread the disease, generally believed to be bubonic plague. Their bite attacked the lymphatic system, and one in three sufferers died within a fortnight. Daniel Defoe, writing in his *Journal of the Plague Year*, describes the dreadful scenes:

> Some were immediately overwhelmed with violent fevers, vomitings, insufferable headaches and pains in the back, with ravings and ragings: others with swellings and tumours in the neck or groin or armpits, which, till they could be broke, put them into insufferable agonies and torment;

Jack Sheppard, who returned the St Giles' bowl half full.

> while others were silently infected, they seeing little of it till they fell into swooning, and faintings, and death without pain.

People tried to ward off the pestilence by wearing amulets or charms, even carrying a piece of paper with the word 'abracadabra' written on it. Unscrupulous quacks pedalled cures such as 'anti-pestilential pills' or the 'Royal Antidote'. Samuel Pepys, in his diary, notes that he was given a bottle of 'plague water'. None of the cures were effective, and some were actually harmful; the King's doctor, Sir Charles Scarborough, for example, wrote a *Practical method as used for the cure of the plague* which recommends drinking 'oil of vitriol' (sulphuric acid), scarifying the body 'with deep Gafhes' and then, if that fails, 'to make use of the Actual Cautery, until, in all parts, there be a Senfe of Pain' – quickly afterwards washing off the scabs with a ointment made of 'oyl of scorpions'. Smoking tobacco or soaking clothing and coins in vinegar were also thought to prevent infection. However, many of the prostitutes of Baldwin's Gardens in Holborn erroneously believed themselves immune, by virtue of their having contracted a venereal disease.

At its height over a 1,000 people a month died in St Giles. The wealthy left as soon as they could; the sick and the poor remained. Defoe wrote:

> I went up Holborn, and there the street was full of people, but they walked in the middle of the great street, neither on one side or the other, because they would not mingle with anybody that came out of houses, or meet smells and scent from the houses that might be infected.

Londoners were desperate to hide their symptoms, for when a family member fell ill the authorities began to shut up houses, this time for forty days. A red cross was painted on the door, with the words 'LORD HAVE MERCY UPON US' in capital letters. The people shut in were terrified, begging to be allowed to leave. Watchmen patrolled the streets but some families managed to escape their boarded-up properties, breaking the locks, escaping over back garden walls or even travelling over the rooftops. Others bribed the watchmen. In Hampstead village, of the 180 persons who died, almost all were local residents. Just a dozen were Londoners, who probably brought the plague with them.

Stories about plague pits have entered London's mythology: in particular, that they were numerous and that their location was subsequently forgotten. Or that certain tube lines in central London curve to avoid them. However, it's now believed that very few were dug. Disposing of the bodies was certainly a problem and large common graves were excavated, often within existing churchyards. St Giles provided the resting place for many victims. Bodies were transported in the dead cart, to the call of 'bring out your dead', and burials were restricted to the hours between sunset and sunrise. The story is told of a man who had a lucky escape after he fell asleep on the steps of St Andrew's church, Holborn Hill. Taken for a corpse, he was placed in the cart. Fortunately, his dog's howling was so loud it woke him, saving him from being buried alive.

AD 1678

THE MYSTERIOUS DEATH OF JUSTICE GODFREY

IN 1678, FIFTY-SIX-YEAR-OLD Edmund Berry Godfrey was a prosperous merchant and well-respected magistrate. A single man, he lived in Hartshorn Lane (now Northumberland Avenue) with his secretary, a housekeeper and a maid. Edmund came from an old Kentish family. He was knighted for his fearless work during the Great Plague and the Fire of London: when many people left the city he stayed, despite the danger.

This was the time of the Restoration of the Monarchy after Cromwell; Charles II was King and his brother James was the Duke of York. Although Charles favoured religious tolerance, many influential people held strongly anti-Catholic views. In September 1678 Titus Oates and Israel Tonge, two fanatical anti-Catholics, went to Justice Godfrey to swear, on oath, that their allegation of a Popish or Catholic plot to overthrow the King was true. They produced a document purporting to give details of the conspiracy. In fact, it was a pack of lies. The document was shown to the King and his most senior advisers, the Privy Council, on 28 September. Charles dismissed the allegations and

left for Newmarket to attend the races. But the Lords believed Oates: they issued warrants, and Oates was given command of a force of officers to arrest the people he had named.

It was such a volatile situation that Godfrey became concerned for his personal safety. He was last seen alive on 12 October. Five days later, a discovery was made by two men walking through the rain towards the White House, later renamed the Chalk Farm tavern. As they skirted a ditch at the bottom of Primrose Hill they noticed a cane, a belt and pair of gloves but took no further notice. However, when they told the landlord he went with them to investigate. A short search revealed a dreadful sight: the body of a man facedown in the bramble-covered ditch, impaled on a sword that was sticking out 8in through his back. It was Sir Edmund Berry Godfrey. The inquest produced some startling facts. Godfrey had been strangled before the sword was plunged through his body – and despite the muddy ground, his shoes were clean. It seemed certain, therefore, that he'd been killed elsewhere, his body taken to Primrose Hill and dumped. This theory gained strength when cart tracks

The murder of Godfrey as represented in the Gentleman's Magazine.

Somerset House (seen here at a later date), where the body of Godfrey was allegedly seen.

were found close by the ditch. Word quickly spread through the country that Godfrey had been murdered by the Catholics, which of course suggested that Oates was right: 'the murder proved the Plot, the Plot the murder.'

The King offered a reward of £500 (over £60,000 today) for the discovery of the murderers, and a pardon to any of the murderers who informed on the rest. This huge sum brought forward 'discoverers', people who claimed they knew what had happened. The first was William Bedloe, who said he'd been offered £4,000 by the Jesuits if he would join five other men to kill a man at Somerset House. This was the home of Charles's Catholic Queen Catherine and was a well-known Catholic refuge and gathering place. Bedloe gave the Privy Council the names of three men he said had been involved; further, he claimed that he'd actually seen the body of Godfrey at Somerset House, though he had not, he insisted, been directly involved in Godfrey's death. This was a complex fabrication, but it was just what the Lords wanted to hear. In October and December, the first Catholics were hanged, drawn and quartered at Tyburn. The next of the discoverers was Miles Prance, a Catholic silversmith. He accused three men who worked at Somerset House, Robert Green, Henry

Berry and Lawrence Hill, of being the murderers. They were tried, found guilty and executed.

Many innocent men lost their lives as a result of the widespread fear of a Catholic revolution. While the Popish Plot was a fabrication, there were real grounds for suspicion. In 1670, at the secret Treaty of Dover, Charles had agreed to support King Louis of France in return for money, promising England would adopt the Catholic faith at a later date.

Godfrey's death has been called the greatest unsolved crime in history, and numerous theories have been put forward to explain what happened. One view was suicide by self-strangulation, but a modern re-examination by a Home Office pathologist, Keith Simpson, showed this was not really possible. He may indeed have been killed by Catholics because of his Protestant beliefs (or by supporters of Oates and Tonge if he knew the plot was a fabrication).

Stephen Knight (1984) showed that Godfrey was a member of a small group working under Sir Robert Peyton. Peyton was part of the Green Ribbon Club, whose members were aware of the Treaty of Dover. Unable to confront the King directly, instead they plotted to replace Charles with a republic, headed by Cromwell's son Richard. Knight believed that Godfrey had told a close Catholic friend, Edward Coleman, to escape before he could be arrested, and that he was killed by members of the Green Ribbon Club for his betrayal. This is one of the more likely theories, but there is no definitive answer.

Sir Edmund was buried at St Martin-in-the-Fields, where the priest reading the funeral sermon declared, 'his death was untimely, and bloody, and treacherous.' The grave no longer exists, but there is a memorial to Edmund and his brother Edward in Westminster Abbey.

AD 1700s

STAND AND DELIVER!

THERE ARE SOME actual reports, and many more unsubstantiated stories, of robberies by highwaymen and footpads in Camden. In the days before street lights and policemen, the roads out of London were dangerous places. There were no banks, so people often carried large sums of money. Hampstead Heath came in for its fair share of attacks but wasn't as popular with robbers as Hounslow Heath or Finchley Common. It was a foolish man who dared to ride alone. From the 1100s until the Dissolution of the Monasteries, travellers were given food and rest at Kilburn Priory, close to the Edgware Road. They gathered in groups, to continue their journey along Shoot-Up Hill and the forest of Middlesex, hoping by virtue of numbers to deter robbers. This was the pilgrimage route to the very popular shrine of St Albans.

Dick Turpin, who mainly plied his trade in Essex, was also associated with Kilburn Wells (near the old Priory) and the Spaniards Inn on Hampstead Heath. It was said he kept his horse, Black Bess, at the tavern and had spare keys to the stables and tollgate nearby, allowing him to escape pursuers. Innkeepers were known to work with thieves. However, these local links are completely fictional: they have been taken from William Harrison Ainsworth's 1834 book *Rookwood*. Ainsworth, who lived in Kilburn, made Dick Turpin's exploits appear heroic, but in reality he was a violent criminal, who thought little of torturing his victims over an open fire. *Rookwood* included Dick's famous but impossible ride on Black Bess, covering the 200 miles from London to York in under a day. Turpin was hanged at York in 1739. Highwaymen also feature in Samuel Richardson's novel *Clarissa* (1748). Clarissa eludes her captor Lovelace in Hampstead, but is deterred from further escape by stories of highwaymen, including a dreadful robbery nearby.

In Defoe's (1722) fictional autobiography of the highwayman Colonel Jack, the hero describes robbing Mrs Smith of Kentish Town. About an hour before sunset, Jack and his partner Will decide to stake out the road towards St Pancras Old Church, 'to observe any chance game, which they might shoot flying.' They stop a party of travellers there. Jack stopped two

'Colonel Jack'. The church is in the background of the engraving. (Courtesy of Camden Local Studies and Archive Centre)

women: 'Speaking to the elderly nurse I said, don't be in such haste, don't be frightened sweetheart said I to the maid, a little of that money in the bottom of your pocket, will make all easy and I'll do you no harm.' When the women started screaming, Jack advised, 'Make no noise, unless you have a mind to force us to murder you!' He robbed the younger woman of 5s 6d and the nurse, 22s, all she had in the world. Although Jack claims, 'it made my heart bleed to see her agony' and asks her name, he still keeps her money. He later decides to give up crime, and goes to Kentish Town to repay the cash. Jack concludes his story by relating how he escaped the hangman's noose when he was included in a general pardon.

Supposedly Platts Lane off Finchley Road was originally called Duval's Lane after a famous French highwayman,

Claude Duval. But there are no reports of his activities in the neighbourhood. He gained a reputation as a ladies' man, but in truth he was little more than a serial womaniser. A much-repeated story concerns a coach robbery, where Duval danced with a lady passenger and, in return, reduced the amount of money he stole from her companion. The incident was painted by William Powell Frith. Duval was just twenty-six years old when he was hanged at Tyburn in 1670. His body was viewed by huge crowds when it was exhibited at the Tangier Tavern in St Giles, Holborn. Many, if not most, of the mourners at his funeral in the Covent Garden church were women, and his epitaph was said to read:

Here lies Du Vall: Reader if male thou art,
Look to thy purse; if female, to thy heart.

In 1673, highwayman Francis Jackson and his four companions fought their final battle near North End, Hampstead. After a series of robberies they had been pursued across country, and it was reported that 200 men lined up against them. After running Henry Miller through with a sword, Francis Jackson was captured and, along with the survivors of his gang, sentenced to be hanged. The route to Tyburn from Newgate Prison lay along Holborn Hill, past the church of St Giles and along Oxford Street. Thousands of people watched the condemned man's last journey. In an effort to deter other malefactors, it was customary to display the body close to the scene of the crime. Jackson's chained corpse was hung from a beam between two elms by the

PELTED TO DEATH FOR PERJURY

On 13 June 1732, John Waller was put in the pillory at Seven Dials, St Giles-in-the-Fields. The pillory was a wooden framework on a post, with holes for the head and hands, in which offenders were locked. On several occasions Waller had falsely accused persons of robbing him, in order to claim the reward given out for information resulting in the capture of a felon. Two or three minutes after being locked in place, he was 'most furiously pelted with large stones, pieces of bottles and colliflower (*sic*) stalks.' His face and head were badly cut. Then Edward Dalton – whose brother, John, had been executed on the strength of Waller's evidence – and his friend Richard Griffith pulled Waller down and tore off all his clothes, save his stockings and shoes. The two men then 'beat Waller and kicked him and jumped upon him till they killed him'. It was a brutal attack that went on for well over fifteen minutes. 'He was bruised all over. His head was beat quite flat; no features could be seen in his face.' Waller was buried at St Andrew Holborn, and Griffith and Dalton were executed for his murder.

The pillory in action. As can be seen from this image (showing Londoner James Egan, who was killed whilst locked into the contraption), cuts and wounds to the face and body were extremely common.

road leading to North End. For the next eighteen years, the grisly sight of his suspended skeleton scared many unwary travellers. The beam was supposed to have been turned into a mantleshelf for a kitchen in Jack Straw's Castle, a nearby public house.

In the eighteenth century, Londoners in search of a cure or just wanting entertainment flocked to Hampstead Wells or Belsize House, off Haverstock Hill, where food, gambling and dancing were all available. The Wells' authorities were forced to place advertisements informing customers that at 10.30 p.m. every Monday, Thursday and Saturday nights, 'there will be a sufficient guard to attend the company thence to London.' Likewise, for the 'Security of his Guests' the owner of Belsize provided 'twelve stout fellows to prevent the Insults of Highwaymen or Footpads.' Their number was later increased to thirty. In 1756, it was arranged that two armed men would escort Kentish Town residents to and from Bloomsbury on winter evenings, but even that was not enough: in 1761, one man committed five robberies on a single day on the road from Highgate to Kentish Town. Continuing problems led to the passing of 'Lighting and Watching' Acts, to provide travellers with better security.

AD 1746

THE HEADLESS JACOBITES OF BLOOMSBURY

ON 3 AUGUST 1746, the bodies of eight headless Jacobites were interred in the burial ground of St George the Martyr and St George Bloomsbury, close to the Foundling Hospital. Their heads were publically displayed to deter followers of the Jacobite cause.

Named after the Latin for James, the Jacobites were fighting to restore the Stuarts to the English throne instead of the Hanoverian Kings. They raised an army to depose the King, but it was not to be: the army of the Young Pretender, Charles Edward Stuart, popularly known as 'Bonnie Prince Charlie', was forced to flee to Scotland, and the final remnants of his troops in England were crammed into a dungeon in Carlisle Castle without food or water.

The commander of that army, Francis Townley, and his officers were moved

Carlisle Castle, where the Jacobites were held in the dungeons. (LC-DIG-ppmsc-08096)

Scenes from the life of 'Butcher' Cumberland, who accepted the Bloomsbury Jacobites' surrender and then sent them to their awful deaths. The axeman and the gallows can be seen at the bottom left. Every enemy soldier found on the battlefield at Culloden was slaughtered, gaining him the soubriquet. (LC-USZ62-76314)

to London and tried for treason at Southwark on 15 July 1746. He and eight others were found guilty and sentenced to be hanged, drawn and quartered on 30 July, at Kennington Common, near Camberwell. In addition to Townley they were: George Fletcher and John Berwick, both linen drapers; Thomas Chadwick, a tallow maker; James Dawson, a student at Cambridge; Thomas Deacon, the son of a minister; Andrew Blood, a gentleman's steward; Thomas Siddal, a Manchester barber; and David Morgan, a lawyer.

At their trials, the men were described as wearing white cockades, and plaid waistcoats or sashes, all signifying their support for the Pretender's cause. The clergyman who visited the prisoners said:

> From the time of their condemnation, a decent cheerfulness constantly appeared in their countenances and behaviour. The near approach of a violent death, armed with the utmost terror of pain and torments, made no impression of dread upon their minds.

Chadwick was a talented musician who did his best to amuse his companions. On the morning of the 30th, 'he declared that although his time drew near he was as hearty as ever he had been in his life, nor was he sorry for what he had done, for if it was to do again he would act in the same manner.' Dawson also declared that even if they'd weighed him down with a ton of iron chains, 'it would not in the least affect his resolution.' Fletcher said that his death was his own fault: his mother had offered him £1,000 not to volunteer.

When their irons had been knocked off, their arms were tied behind their backs, ropes put around their necks and the men were loaded onto three sledges. Fifteen hundred troops escorted the procession to the Common, where a viewing scaffold had been erected and an enormous crowd had gathered. The executioner – who had hired three assistants 'for the quicker dispatch of [the] business' – rode in the first sledge. The prisoners weren't allowed a clergyman, but David Morgan led the group in prayers for half an hour. Before the sentence was carried out, the men threw their hats and prayer books into the crowd as well as their written speeches, saying they died in a just cause. Then the barbaric execution got underway.

Right, above *Death to Jacobites: the block on which many of London's Jacobites lost their heads – including Lord Lovat, another Jacobite (who perished the following year). He was the last British man to die in this manner. (LC-USZ61-922)*

Right, below *Heads on Temple Bar.*

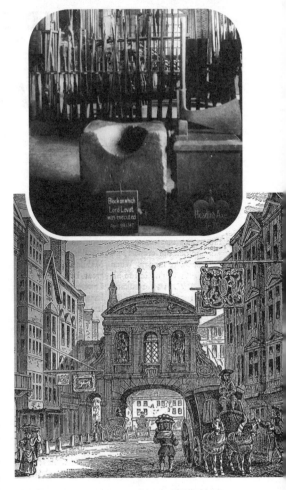

Each man had a cap pulled over his eyes and was hanged for three minutes, a time specified by the treason law of Edward III. This short time meant that the condemned was often still alive when cut down, as indeed was the intention; Townley certainly showed some signs of consciousness. They were then stripped, disembowelled, had their entrails thrown onto a fire and beheaded. Finally, their bodies were cut into four quarters by the executioner, who cried, 'God save King George!' The remains were put on the sledges and taken back to prison. The heads of Townley and Fletcher were displayed on pikes at Temple Bar for many years. Townley's head was recovered in secret, but only interred in the family crypt at Townley Hall, Lancashire, in 1945. Siddal and Deacon were displayed on the Manchester Exchange. Chadwick and Berwick's heads were sent to Carlisle, where they were put up on poles above the English Gate.

On 31 July, Townley's body was placed in a vault in St Pancras churchyard. On 3 August the other eight men were interred in one grave in the burial ground behind the Foundling Hospital, now known as St George's Gardens. Five other Jacobites who were executed and beheaded at Kennington Common are also buried here. Donald MacDonald, James Nicolson and Walter Ogilvie, who died on 22 August, were 'decently interred' in a single grave. They were transported in three separate hearses, attended by mourning coaches. In this case, bodies and severed heads were reunited and buried together. Captain James Bradshaw and John Hamilton, the governor of Carlisle Castle, were executed on 30 November.

Bonnie Prince Charlie's escape after the Battle of Culloden (1746) – with the help from Flora MacDonald, who disguised him as her maid – has become a legend and is remembered in the Skye Boat song. The Prince returned to France and remained in exile, dying in Rome on 31 January 1788.

AD 1832

GOING A-FISHING

The Work of the Resurrection Men

UNTIL THE 1832 Anatomy Act was passed, the bodies of murderers condemned to death and dissection provided the only legal source of corpses for anatomical research. But there just weren't enough to satisfy demand. Corpses became a commodity, to be stolen and sold. As long as nothing was removed, such as clothes or jewellery, the theft of a body was only punishable by a fine or imprisonment. Some thought it well worth the risk and didn't care how they carried out their grim work. The price paid for an adult corpse rose from one or two guineas at the end of the eighteenth century to as much as eight, ten or even sixteen guineas by 1828 (today worth an astonishing £1,000). 'Smalls' – in other words, children – were charged by the inch.

Several of the private medical schools played an important role in advancing the science of anatomy, notably those run by Dr William Hunter in Great Windmill Street and Dr Joshua Brookes in Blenheim Street, close to Oxford Street. But they had no access to corpses and had to buy them. So when Dr Brookes spoke up for a known grave robber in 1814, was he trying to protect his supplier? 'Mr Brookes expressed the hope that the prisoner might be discharged, as he was, in fact, a necessary individual in the promotion of surgery.' In 1823 he wrote a letter to the Secretary of State where he freely admitted how he acquired corpses, mentioning that in the last month the police had seized three bodies 'for which I had paid large sums'.

Inside William Hunter's Hunterian Museum at the Royal College of Surgeons in the 1830s. (LC-USZ62-107136)

Brookes pressed for reform. An 1828 Select Committee concluded that the law needed changing, and this ultimately led to the passing of the 1832 Act. But for the bereaved, who wanted their loved ones to stay buried, the Resurrection Men were among the most hated members of society. Three Resurrection Men gave evidence to the Select Committee. Charles Dickens wrote a fearsome description of them, declaring that they were:

> ...some of the strangest and vilest beings that have perhaps ever visited such respectable places. Sallow, cadaverous, gaunt men. Their ghoulish faces were rendered horrible by smirks of self-satisfied cunning, and their eyes squinted with sidelong suspicion, fear and distrust. These were vampires who earned their bread in a horrible way.

One witness claimed that between 1809 and 1813 he was the sole supplier of subjects to the London anatomy schools. 'According to my book,' he said, 'I provided upwards of 1,200 adult bodies and over 150 small subjects under three feet.' The price was then four guineas for an adult. Dickens wrote, 'There were terrible rumours that when "subjects" ran short, they had a way of making dead bodies.' An eminent surgeon writing in *The Times* in 1831 said that paying for corpses was an inducement to murder, and the dissection, which meant the bodies were disfigured, removed all evidence of the crime. Some Resurrection Men appeared respectable, going about their work 'so privately that nobody knows anything about it'. Another witness to the Select Committee said just three men made a

regular living from raising bodies, with the remainder, perhaps as many as 200, making an occasional snatch and generally working in gangs – the most bodies in one go being an astonishing twenty-three over four nights. Many robbers lived close to King's Cross, where the Golden Lion pub in Gray's Inn Road was a favourite meeting place.

St Pancras churchyard on Pancras Road was very isolated and popular with the snatchers. Jonathan Wild was an obvious target, a mastermind who worked on both sides of the law for years. He was hanged in 1725 and buried in St Pancras; his empty coffin was found a few days later, at the corner of Crowndale Road.

In 1750, the landlord of a nearby tavern watched in horror as a robber made off with a woman's corpse slung

Jonathan Wild going to his death, pelted by the crowds.

In 1840, the *Weekly Dispatch* reported that the skeleton of Wild was 'in the possession of Mr Fowler, surgeon, of Sheet Street, Windsor', handed down from its original owner, a London surgeon named Brand who was 'on terms of intimacy with the Ordinary of Newgate at the time of Wilde's [*sic*] execution'. The original coffin plate, 'of thin sheet iron, very much corroded with rust', was attached to the front of the skeleton's display case. The skull, which was sent to a phrenologist in the Strand, allegedly suggested a person 'very likely to commit crime'. Dr Fowler presented the skeleton to the Royal College of Surgeons, and it can be seen today in the Hunterian Museum.

Ticket to the execution of Wild.

over his back. St Pancras appointed watchmen, armed with a blunderbuss, and later added fierce dogs. The record of a gang working in 1812 reveals a horrendous haul: on 20 February, fifteen large bodies and one child were taken; in March, a total of eighteen adults, two children and two foetuses. Five adults and a child were lifted on 25 November, and on 2 December, another six adults, one child and a foetus. Charles Dickens describes the work of the Resurrection Men in the churchyard in *A Tale of Two Cities*, calling the gruesome act 'going a-fishing'.

The earliest charge of grave robbing was made in 1777. The corpse was taken from the St George Bloomsbury burial ground (where the headless Jacobites of the previous chapter were buried). The gravedigger and his assistant were convicted of stealing the body of Mrs Jane Sainsbury. She was discovered in a sack, 'with the heels tied up tight behind her, the hands tied together behind, with cords round the neck, so as almost forcibly to bend the neck between the legs.' In 1798, a watchman disturbed robbers in the graveyard of Whitefield's Tabernacle on Tottenham Court Road. They fled, leaving behind their 'dead stock': eight corpses tied up in sacks and a child's body, already loaded into a coach. The coachman, who was captured, had previously been implicated in a robbery from Hampstead churchyard.

Where possible, relatives would mount guard over a grave, until natural decay meant the corpse was no longer suitable for the dissecting table. Such precautions were justified, as officials frequently accepted bribes from the body snatchers. In 1822 the watchman at St Pancras was found guilty of helping the Resurrection Men by preventing his guard dogs from attacking them. However, Mrs Garratty, the widow of a King's Cross chimney sweep, didn't trust the watchman. Taunted by the snatchers, who informed her that they planned to take her husband's body, she came up with a clever solution: she made friends with the dogs before her husband was buried. She then sat and guarded his grave for nine lonely nights, armed only with a poker, stopping the snatchers from carrying out their threat.

The graves of the poor presented an easier target because their bodies were not buried as deep as those of the rich. But in St Andrew's Holborn burial ground, in Shoe Lane, considerable precautions were taken. A hole for 100 paupers' coffins was protected by a large piece of iron, winched up when necessary, with an iron bar across flaps to the hole, secured by a massive padlock. First the plate was stolen, and four bodies taken; next, the robbers returned and replaced the padlock with one of their own. When the substitution was discovered, a watch was mounted.

Body snatchers in action!

At 1.30 a.m., four men came over the wall. After opening their lock, two got into the hole. The sexton promptly closed the flaps and locked them in!

As a Resurrection Man, Israel Chapman 'stood at the head of his profession'. Charles Dickens wrote that he 'bought bodies off sextons and sold dead people's teeth to dentists'. Israel lived in the Haymarket, and later in Vine Street, Covent Garden, and ran a large gang of snatchers. He confessed his gang 'raised from their graves as many as fifty bodies in a week'. Chapman was known for dividing corpses into portions and selling off each part, and was credited with the idea of stealing bodies before they were buried. In 1818 he made the mistake of diversifying into highway robbery. He was caught and sentenced to be hanged. It seemed that he was destined, somewhat ironically, to become a victim of the snatchers, but then his sentence was commuted to transportation to Australia. There Chapman married. He was appointed constable in the prison lumber yard, and carried out his duties so well that he eventually earned a conditional pardon and joined the Sydney police. He excelled here too, and obtained a full pardon in 1827. In 1829 he sailed for England but returned to Australia in 1832, where he continued his successful police career until his death in 1868.

THE MARVELLOUS BOY

Shoe Lane cemetery's inhabitants also included the poet described by William Wordsworth as the 'marvellous boy, the sleepless soul that perished in its pride.'

Born in Bristol in 1752, Thomas Chatterton was first employed as a legal writer, working twelve hours a day. His employer said that Thomas had a 'sullen and gloomy temper' and his family described him as often withdrawn, in a world of his own. Chatterton was already deeply interested in the medieval period and was fascinated by boxes of old manuscripts that his father had rescued from a local church, St Mary Redcliffe. This inspired Thomas and gave him the means to compose the writings of a monk, 'Thomas Rowley'. He claimed his father had recovered the monk's papers from the Bristol church, 'but no Thomas Rowley ever existed in this incarnation: he was the brilliant, compelling, and perplexing creature of Chatterton's brain.' He produced a mammoth amount of 'Rowley work': plays, poetry, letters and reports. These forgeries were very carefully crafted and accurately written pieces, in old handwriting, sometimes on vellum. Chatterton developed an archaic spelling system and compiled a special dictionary to produce an invented language based on existing old texts. Within a year, he had published thirty-one titles (some forgeries, others original work) in seven different journals. He was just seventeen years old.

Chatterton left Bristol for London in late April 1780, planning to work as a freelance writer. He soon came to lodge with Mrs Angell, at 4 (later 39) Brooke Street, Holborn. Mrs Angell, by profession a dressmaker, ran a bawdy house, and Thomas had his own garret room. He probably slept with both his landlady and her girls, and certainly contracted a venereal disease. He dosed himself with medicines bought from Mr Cross, a nearby apothecary. Chatterton died at Brooke Street on the night of 24 August 1870. It was reported that he committed suicide, some citing poverty and professional setbacks as the reason. It has since been argued that his death could have been the result of an accidental overdose – that Chatterton had unwisely mixed his venereal medicine (arsenic) with a recreational drug, opium. His body was taken to the nearby workhouse of St Andrew Holborn, and buried in the paupers' graveyard in Shoe Lane.

The Shoe Lane burial ground no longer exists. When the site was redeveloped the bodies were exhumed, but what happened to Chatterton's remains is not known. The romantic myths concerning Chatterton certainly inspired later generations of poets. Literary critics largely condemned him (and his body of work) for the forgeries, but more recently his important contribution to English literature has been recognised. There is a plaque noting Chatterton's death high up on the side of the current building in Brooke Street.

AD 1780

A TIME OF TERROR

The Gordon Riots

THE DAYS OF the violent 'Anti-Popery' Riots in June 1780, vividly captured in Charles Dickens' novel *Barnaby Rudge*, were among the most lawless and terrifying of London's history.

The riots were provoked by the Relief Act of 1778, which tried to remove some of the official discrimination against Catholics. Two years later, Lord George Gordon, a powerful Protestant who held extreme views, demanded the Act's repeal and whipped up a great deal of anti-Catholic feeling. A series of notices invited his supporters to gather on Friday, 2 June 1780 in St George's Fields, Southwark. An enormous crowd of between 40,000 and 60,000 converged on Parliament to present a petition for the Act to be repealed. Many carried banners declaring 'No Popery' and wore blue cockades, which became the symbol of the movement. Lord Mansfield, one of the main supporters of the Act, was accosted and abused, and the mob only dispersed when a detachment of soldiers arrived. The petition was then dismissed, and officials believed the worst was over. Instead, what followed was a week of virtually unchallenged mob rule.

Lord George Gordon.

That night, two chapels were attacked. Fires were lit, the largest in the middle of Lincoln's Inn Fields. A large, unruly element bent on mischief joined the crowd, mainly drawn from the nearby poor and lawless streets of the St Giles Rookery. On this and subsequent nights, much of the action happened in and around the Holborn area. The homes and businesses of Catholics or people believed to have Catholic sympathies were attacked. Meanwhile, the cry of 'No Popery' was taken up and used as a cover

Newgate Prison in flames.

for criminal damage. Discontentment over falling wages and rising prices also fanned the flames.

On 5 June the rioting continued, as troops generally refused to intervene. The following evening the mob swarmed into Leicester Fields (today's Leicester Square). The cry went up: 'A-hoy for Newgate!' Newgate Prison once stood where the Old Bailey stands today. The mob attacked and destroyed it, pulling down the walls with hooks and releasing all the prisoners, and painting on the walls that the inmates had been freed by order of 'His Majesty, King Mob'. Other prisons were targeted: the nearby Fleet and, on the South Bank, the Clink, King's Bench and Marshalsea were emptied, and all but the last were set

ablaze. Gordon was drawn in his carriage through the streets by the mob, who were whooping and yelling like people possessed. Some terrified Londoners tried to flee, while others painted slogans on their doors or hung out blue flags to signify support for the rioters.

But Black Wednesday, 7 June, was the worst day. In the early hours of the morning, a large mob entered Bloomsbury Square. Lord and Lady Mansfield escaped shortly before looters broke into their home. Everything moveable was thrown into the street and burned, including the irreplaceable contents of his law library. The contents of the wine cellar were 'plentifully bestowed' among the crowd, who used tar-soaked rope to fire the house. The army fired on the mob, killing at least five people. A large group set off, bent on destroying Lord Mansfield's country home, Kenwood, at Highgate. The landlord of the nearby Spaniards Inn plied the rioters with drinks and sent for help, while Lord Mansfield's steward handed out free beer. The militia arrived to find a drunken and disorientated rabble, who returned to London without any bloodshed.

The disorder peaked at around 9 p.m. near Fetter Lane, Holborn, culminating in 'a night of the most dreadful horror'.

'ENCAMPMENT IN BRITISH MUSEUM GARDENS'

The Yorkshire Militia were based in the garden of Montagu House on Great Russell Street (the original British Museum) at the time of the Gordon Riots. The officers had marquees while the privates had tents. The militia stayed encamped in Bloomsbury until early August.

Thomas Langdale was a wealthy Catholic, and his gin distillery had 120,000 gallons on the premises. He'd freely distributed liquor among the rioters in the vain hope it might save his business. It did not. The building was set alight as people tried to collect alcohol in any container they could find. The heat caused the vats to explode, with terrible consequences for those inside, releasing torrents of gin into the street:

Soldiers opening fire on Londoners as the streets burn.

> Spirits, now running to pools and wholly unfit for human consumption, were swallowed by insatiate fiends, who with shrieking gibes and curses, reeled and perished in the flames, whilst others, alight from head to foot, were dragged from burning cellars. Flames leapt upwards and columns of fire became visible for 30 miles round London.

Seven bodies were found in the ruins. Thirty-six major fires were started, and many believed London would be destroyed. The Bank of England was attacked three times. The militia fired on the rioters, killing and wounding many, and during the third attack, Howitzers were used. Slowly, the troops and militias gained the upper hand, and by 9 June normality was returning to the streets.

Around 100 Catholic buildings – churches, businesses and homes – had been attacked or destroyed. The true death toll is unknown: for the rioters, figures range from 300 to as many as 850. Twenty-five rioters were hanged, two or three outside Mansfield's Bloomsbury house.

Lord Gordon, the instigator, was arrested and charged with high treason. Ironically, the judge at his trial was Lord Mansfield. Gordon was found 'not guilty'; he later converted to Judaism, and died in Newgate Prison in 1793. He was buried in the graveyard of St James's, Hampstead Road. When Newgate was demolished in 1901, Madame Tussauds bought Gordon's cell and reassembled it in the 'Chamber of Horrors', with a tableaux showing Gordon inside, dying from gaol fever.

PISTOLS AT DAWN

DUELLING HAS A long history. It was not finally outlawed in England until the middle of the nineteenth century. Even after this time, people would travel to the Continent to resolve their affairs of honour.

One of the most publicised duels in Camden occurred on 6 April 1803. Colonel Montgomery was taking his daily ride in Rotten Row, Hyde Park, with his large Newfoundland dog 'Wolf' following his horse. Riding nearby was Captain MacNamara, accompanied by his dog, also a Newfoundland. The animals began to fight – and the

Colonel's younger and smaller dog was clearly getting the worst of it. Getting off his horse to separate them, Montgomery declared that he'd knock the other dog down if it attacked again; 'if you knock my dog down you must knock me down afterwards,' replied the furious Captain.

The two arranged to resolve the dispute with a duel. They settled on that same day at Primrose Hill, a well-known duelling spot. Two hours later, at 7 p.m., both parties and their seconds arrived in coaches. Captain MacNamara sent to ask if the Colonel would apologise, but he refused. The men then each

Duelling: the great trial of nerves. (D.T. Egerton, 1824, courtesy of Camden Local Studies and Archive Centre)

Rotten Row, where the encounter took place. (LC-DIG-ppmsc-08575)

selected a pistol, took 'twelve very long paces' (about 15 yards), and, when the signal was given, fired. The Colonel fell to the ground, shot through the heart. The Captain was wounded above his hip. The Colonel was taken to the Chalk Farm tavern, but died within minutes of arriving. At the inquest, the coroner's jury recorded a verdict of manslaughter, rather than murder, and MacNamara was tried at the Old Bailey on 22 October. Lord Hood and Lord Nelson, who had known MacNamara about eight years, gave evidence of his good character. The jury retired for about twenty minutes and found MacNamara, who had not intended to kill his rival, not guilty. It was later said that neither man had anything to prove: 'two braver men whose courage was better known, did not exist. What passed respecting the dogs might have been honourably explained and adjusted had the parties slept on the quarrel.'

One of the last duels in England took place on 1 July 1843. Lieutenant Alexander Thompson Munro and Lieutenant-Colonel David Lynar Fawcett had married two sisters, Eliza and Anne Porter, and were thus brothers-in-law. Munro, aged thirty-nine, lived in Brompton Square, and Fawcett nearby, in Sloane Street. He was thirty-four and had a young family. Fawcett had recently returned from service in China. In his absence Munro had looked after his affairs, but Fawcett was unhappy with Munro's handling of a house sale. Munro issued a challenge to fight, and at 5 a.m. the parties met in a field adjoining the rifle ground of the Brecknock Arms on Camden Road.

The toll-keeper of the gate opposite was surprised at seeing the gentlemen

Montgomery and MacNamara fight.

so early in the morning. When he heard a shot he told a police constable that he thought a duel had taken place. The constable arrived at the spot to find Colonel Fawcett bleeding from a wound in the chest. When asked what had happened, Fawcett replied, 'What is that to you? It is an accident.' He complained of the cold, but in the absence of the owner a waiter refused to allow the wounded man to be taken inside the Brecknock Arms. Instead, Fawcett was carried about half a mile to the Camden Arms, Randolph Street. There, despite the attention of two highly skilled surgeons, he died two days later. Before passing out, Fawcett said he wished he'd been killed in action.

Attitudes had changed in the forty years since the Primrose Hill duel. This time the inquest jury brought in a verdict of 'wilful murder' against Munro and his seconds. The coroner was Thomas Wakley, founder of *The Lancet*. The seconds, Lieutenants Cuddy and Grant, were tried at the Old Bailey but found not guilty. Alexander Munro avoided justice by fleeing to the

Lieutenant Munro.

Continent and joining the Prussian Army. In December 1843 the contents of his house in Brompton Square were about to be sold when Thomas Wakley stopped the auction, much to the annoyance of all attending. After four years abroad, Munro eventually returned and surrendered himself to stand trial. On 14 August 1847 he was found guilty and sentenced to death. However, as the jury gave a strong recommendation of mercy, his sentence was commuted to twelve months' imprisonment, but his military career was ruined. The two wives and Lieutenant Munro wrote letters that were published in the papers. Munro said Fawcett had insulted him, an apology from the Colonel or a 'meeting' being the only options. Eliza backed her husband, saying the military friends he consulted 'were of the opinion that there was no other course to be adopted but the one he followed.' Anne Fawcett said her husband had acted reasonably and tried to avoid the duel. As he left the house, he told her, 'I will never fire at your sister's husband.' For both sisters the duel was a tragedy: as Anne put it, it entailed, 'the destruction of the prospects for myself and child, and the utter ruin of every happiness to me.' Due to the nature of his death she was not eligible for an army pension. When Munro fled England he lost his commission, and his wife Eliza was left with their six children.

This duel caused a great public outcry. *The Times* declared that 'duelling has become generally ridiculous, and when not ridiculous, hateful, and requires but a blow from authority to become a crime of a past age.' It led to the establishment of the Anti-Duelling Association, and in 1844 duelling was banned in the army. Eventually pressure from Queen Victoria, who was particularly upset by the Fawcett duel, along with the press and public opinion, led to the more vigorous prosecution for murder and eventually duelling stopped. The last recorded fight took place in 1845.

In 2011, the Camden Arms pub was re-named the 'Colonel Fawcett' in memory of its unfortunate guest.

THE PRIME MINISTER HAS BEEN ASSASSINATED!

AT 5.15 P.M. on Monday, 11 May 1812, a tall, thin man was waiting quietly in the lobby of the House of Commons. The business that evening was a debate about the effect of the embargo on French trade, and only sixty MPs were in the building. Spencer Perceval, the Prime Minister, who was due to speak, was late. As he entered the lobby, the quiet man stood up and drew a small pistol from inside his coat. He walked towards Perceval and fired a single shot at close range, hitting him in the chest. There was a shocked silence: the onlookers were temporarily stunned by the bright flash, loud noise and smell of gunpowder. Then the Prime Minister staggered forward, before falling to the ground, calling out, 'I am murdered!' Perceval was carried to the speaker's apartments, where he was pronounced dead by a local surgeon.

In the meantime, several men grabbed the assailant, who offered no resistance. They seized the pistol, and found another one, fully loaded, in his pocket. He calmly told them his name was John Bellingham and that he shot Perceval 'because of a denial of justice on the part of the Government.'

Bellingham shooting the Prime Minister.

THE VICTIM

Spencer Perceval is chiefly remembered because he is still the only English Prime Minister who has been assassinated. He was born in London in 1762, the son of John Perceval, an Irish MP who inherited the title of the Earl of Egmont and then became Lord Lovel and Holland. The family home was in Charlton, Kent. Spencer studied law and was called to the Bar in 1786. He and his older brother Charles fell in love with a pair of sisters, the daughters of Sir Thomas Spencer-Wilson, who was Lord of the manors of Charlton and Hampstead. In 1787 Charles married Margaretta Wilson, but Spencer, with poorer prospects, was denied her sister Jane. When she turned twenty-one in 1790, however, the couple secretly married and went on to have six sons and six daughters. Perceval advanced rapidly in political circles, holding several important government posts.

In 1800 he bought Nos 59 and 60 Lincoln's Inn Fields (where there is today a blue plaque to his memory). Two years earlier he leased a country home, the large Belsize House, in what was then rural Hampstead. The property was in poor condition; Spencer called it 'a miserable hole' and embarked on renovations and improvements. During his time at Belsize, Perceval took an active part in Hampstead affairs and Perceval Avenue, off Belsize Lane, is named after him. The family left Belsize in 1807 for Elm Grove, another large property in Ealing, and Perceval became Prime Minister the following year.

THE ASSASSIN

John Bellingham was born about 1770 in St Neots, Huntington, and by 1779 the family was living in London. When he was fourteen, John was apprenticed to a jeweller but he ran away to sea. After surviving a mutiny and a shipwreck, he decided on a quieter life as a clerk in London. Following a visit to Archangel, he set up as a broker in Liverpool, arranging insurance for companies importing and exporting goods to Russia.

In 1803, the ship *Sojus* sank in the White Sea. It was owned by wealthy Russian merchants, one of whom was the Mayor of Archangel. Although the ship was insured by Lloyds of London,

John Bellingham.

the company refused to pay: they'd received an anonymous letter saying that the ship had been sabotaged by its owners. The Russian owners believed the letter had been sent by John Bellingham (which he vehemently denied), and plotted their revenge. In 1804, when Bellingham, his young wife and son were in Archangel, he was accused of non-payment of an outstanding debt. He was held in prison, on and off, for the next five years without trial, and his many appeals to the English Embassy for help were ignored. He was finally able to return to England in December 1809, a bitter and angry man.

His wife Mary was living in Liverpool, but Bellingham stayed in London, lodging at No. 53 Theobalds Road and later No. 9 New Millman Street, Bloomsbury, determined to obtain financial compensation from the government. He petitioned a number of people, including Spencer Perceval, with no success. In April 1812 he paid gunsmith W. Beckwith of No. 58 Skinner Street four guineas for a pair of short-barrelled pistols. He practised firing them on Hampstead Heath and, on 12 May, walked to Westminster, where he assassinated the Prime Minister.

TRIAL AND EXECUTION

Bellingham appeared for trial at the Old Bailey on 15 May, only four days after the murder. One of the prosecution team was William Garrow (star character in the recent television series *Garrow's Law*). Bellingham conducted his own defence, which was the standard procedure at the time; counsel was only allowed to assist on points of law. He spoke for over an hour, detailing what had happened in Russia and how no one would help him. He was sorry Perceval was dead, and had no personal grudge against him. If he'd seen Lord Gower, who had been the British Ambassador in Russia, he'd have shot him instead. The jury took just fourteen minutes to return a verdict of 'guilty of murder'.

For Bellingham it was all over inside a week: crime, prosecution and death. It was raining on the morning of 18 May, as a huge crowd began gathering at Newgate Prison. Even Lord Byron stayed awake all night to see Bellingham 'launched into eternity'. Bellingham walked calmly up the steps to the gallows, where the noose was put over his head. As the clock struck 8 a.m., the executioner knocked out the supporting bolt and Bellingham dropped down. Out of sight, the executioner's assistants pulled on his legs to shorten his suffering. There followed a 'perfect and awful silence' before the crowd dispersed. The body was left to hang for an hour, before being taken away on a cart to St Bartholomew's Hospital for dissection.

Coinciding with the 200-year anniversary of the assassination, a new book appeared containing a conspiracy theory – that Bellingham was funded by rich merchants who were opposed to Perceval's policy on the embargo of imports, which had affected their business. But there is very little evidence to support this conjecture. Almost certainly, this was the case of an obsessive and angry man who took the law into his own hands, to correct what he saw as a refusal to grant him justice.

THE BEER TSUNAMI

THE HORSESHOE BREWERY was established before 1764 and located where the Dominion Theatre, Tottenham Court Road, stands today. It was bought by (Sir) Henry Meux in 1809. The brewery business known as Meux, Reid & Co. in Liquorpond Street (off Gray's Inn Road) was started by Henry's father Richard and his partner, Mungo Murray. Henry worked there with his brothers Richard and Thomas. Sadly, however, Richard was declared insane, and Henry and Thomas argued over how to run the company. The business was sold, with the Meuxs getting their share of the proceeds – which is when Henry bought the Horseshoe Brewery. Henry's new business prospered, and production increased.

But on 17 October 1814, at 5.30 p.m., disaster struck: an enormous vat burst, sending a tsunami of beer through neighbouring streets. Some were part of St Giles Rookery, a slum of poorly built and densely populated houses.

Large vats were commonplace in London's porter (beer) breweries and several had been installed at Liquorpond Street. Standing 22ft high and filled to within 4in of the top, the Horseshoe vat contained 3,555 barrels of beer – roughly equivalent to 128,000 gallons of liquid. The force of the flood was so great that a wall of the brew house, 25ft high and 22in thick in places, gave way, taking part of the roof as well. The flood swept east and north, collapsing two houses in New Street and sweeping through the back of properties in Great Russell Street. The falling masonry caused further damage. 'The brewery, viewed from the back of these houses, presents an awful appearance,' runs a contemporary source. 'About 20 yards of the wall on the north side, and the roof, form one indiscriminate mass of ruins.' A second vat, containing 2,400 barrels, was also breached, and all but 800 barrels were lost. The brewery was flooded to waist level with beer, and the workers gagged in the suffocating fumes. As people converged on the devastated buildings, some rescuers asked for silence so that the cries of any victims buried in the rubble could be heard.

Early reports feared as many as twenty or thirty people had died or were missing. Not only houses but inhabited cellars nearby were flooded. Some residents saved themselves by

Messrs Meux's Brewery, 1830.

climbing onto tables and cupboards. The final death toll was eight, three of them young children, and would have been much higher had the accident happened later in the evening. Five of the victims lived in New Street. Here a 'wake' was underway for John Saville, the two-year-old son of Ann Saville, when the flood hit the house. It was reduced to rubble, burying and killing four of the mourners. In a neighbouring house, the Banfields had been having tea: mother and one child were washed away and survived, but poor Hannah Banfield died. Described as a 'fine child' aged four years and four months, she suffered dreadful crushing injuries.

In Great Russell Street the flood severely damaged the rear wall of five properties. Mr Goodwin, who ran a poulterer's business at No. 23, 'was sitting at tea with his family, when a dreadful current carried them off through the shop into the street, but fortunately without injury.' Richard Hawes, the landlord of the Tavistock Arms next door (at No. 22), heard a tremendous crash as the rear wall of his pub collapsed. The cellar and taproom rapidly flooded and he fought hard to save himself as the liquid rushed through the house and out into Great Russell Street. It flowed into the basement areas of houses opposite, smashing a passer-by against the iron railings. Hawes' servant, fourteen-year-old Eleanor Cooper, was killed. She was in the back yard scouring pots and buried by falling masonry. That evening her body was found, still standing by the water butt, evidence that disaster had struck swiftly and suddenly.

The chief witness at the inquest was George Crick, the storehouse clerk at the brewery. He reported that one of twenty-two iron hoops securing the burst vat had fallen off about an hour before the accident. This happened frequently so he wasn't unduly worried. But he now believed the rivets holding one or more hoops had burst. Once the flood had subsided, the foundations and supports of the vat were examined and found to be undamaged. And as the beer had been brewing for ten months, fermentation wasn't to blame. The coroner recorded that the victims died, 'by casualty, accidentally and by misfortune'. Local residents were seen collecting the beer or drinking it on the spot but, unlike at Langdale's distillery during the Gordon Riots, such excess appears to have been on a small and non-lethal scale.

Meux was variously reported as losing between £15,000 and £23,000 (£800,000 to £1,250,000 today), and the brewery was excused the excise duty due on the beer flood. The one large vat at the Horseshoe Brewery was replaced by seven smaller ones and the business continued on-site until 1921.

AD 1819

THE DESPERADOES OF WEST END FAIR

IN 1800 THE rural parish of Hampstead lay some 2 miles beyond the built-up area of London. West End was an isolated village of twenty or so cottages with a farm and a handful of large houses, centred on the area around the present West End Green in West Hampstead.

Like many of its counterparts, West End Fair began by providing simple, largely local entertainment, and then grew into an annual event held over three days in late July. With the arrival of professional entertainers came a substantial increase in the numbers attending, and a marked rise in the consumption of alcohol.

In 1812 the fair experienced its first reported violent incident when 'the Clown of Saunder's Troop of Equestrian Performers' died from wounds inflicted during a fight. But this was an isolated tragedy, perhaps the result of too much alcohol, and the fair continued to present its usual 'scene of mirth and festivity'. It was not to last.

Four years later the fair had expanded to comprise some fifty to sixty wooden, canvas-covered booths, and by 1819 the fair had expanded into a field off Mill Lane, then a rough track that linked the village to Shoot-Up Hill in Kilburn. This allowed the covered booths to be laid out as at other venues, facing each other to form 'streets'. The first day, Monday 26 July, passed off peacefully until early evening. Then the numbers of families declined, leaving younger couples or single men and women to enjoy an evening's fun. Instead, sections of the crowd were 'steamed' – assaulted and robbed by gangs of organised thieves. The gangs clearly knew the event was a soft target, overpowering and outnumbering all who opposed them. Robberies and assaults were also reported in several of the roads and fields nearby. Women screamed as their jewellery was snatched, and many men were beaten to the ground. Clothes, handkerchiefs, hats and shoes were taken, as well as cash and valuables. The assaults took place over several hours and the police were targeted for severe beatings. The first robberies occurred between 6 p.m. and 7 p.m., with a related incident some distance away at the Kilburn turnpike gate (near the present Bell public house). There a group of men attempted to steal the toll money. The

The Bell Inn in 1750. The tollgate can be seen in the distance.

last reported robbery occurred shortly after 11 p.m. The constables and their helpers made some arrests but were vastly outnumbered by the ruffians.

The following report quickly appeared in the newspapers of the day:

> This evening, a most disgraceful and daring scene of riot and plunder took place at West End Fair. Villains in gangs of ten, twenty, or thirty, assaulted, robbed, and rifled every person who they supposed to have money or any valuable articles about them. Knives were used to cut clothing to pieces, and would, if resistance had been offered, been used to silence those resisting. The number of the ruffians had been estimated as high as 200. Many of them were armed with bludgeons; and those who were not tore up the tressels

of the stands for weapons to defend themselves against the police officers and constables.

However, these reports did not appear in the wider press until 29 July, so the next day, Tuesday 27 July, the fair was again well attended, and 'similar outrages, but to a much greater extent, were repeated by the same persons and their associates.' This time the violence erupted later, between 8 p.m. and 9 p.m., and the police made thirty arrests, apprehending many of the thieves inside a drinking booth, which was their main rendezvous and 'the deposit for their booty'.

On 28 July the first men appeared before Bow Street Magistrates' Court. There was a constant stream of witnesses, some badly injured but all anxious to give evidence. A number were too ill to attend, and unfortunately many were unable to identify the men who had robbed them. They told of 'barbarous' beatings by not one but many men, all armed with sticks; of Jay, a Hampstead constable, who was left a broken man who couldn't – or wouldn't – identify his attackers; of women robbed (in one case, the victim having her earlobe cut off to remove an earring).

It emerged that the robberies had been planned by 'acknowledged leaders' of known gangs. A sugar baker by trade, twenty-year-old John Henley was described as 'the Well-Known Captain of the Gang of James-street and Oxford-street robbers'. Henley was the ringleader who attempted to steal the toll money, en route to the fair on the Monday evening.

Five men were sent for trial at the Old Bailey and sentenced to be transported to Australia; John Henley, along with Henry Lovell (aged fifteen) and Edward Cassiday (twenty-one), was sentenced to be hanged. Lovell had confronted Michael Eddington, a law writer from Lincoln's Inn: 'Cut his throat, murder him!' he yelled, before beating Eddington senseless and robbing him. Cassiday had robbed and probably stabbed James Friend, as someone yelled, 'Rip his entrails out!' The wound wasn't serious, but Friend was then battered with a stick. The weapon ended up beneath him when he fell, allowing him to produce the weapon in court. 'We have killed the b--g-r, let him lay in the ditch!' were the last comforting words Cassiday uttered before abandoning Friend to his fate.

The public executions were carried out at Newgate, on the morning of Friday 26 November. John Henley cut a brave figure: the leader was hanged in his curled hair, his velveteen coat, his well-fitting cord knee-britches, his striped stockings, and his brightly polished high-lows (shoes), and was exhibited after execution, at a penny a head, by his affectionate parents in a kitchen in James Street, near Oxford Street.

As a result of the violent events, the wealthier residents of Hampstead got together and made certain the West End Fair was abolished forever.

THE SAVAGE MURDER OF PC GRANTHAM

The First Policeman to Die on Duty

THE METROPOLITAN POLICE Force was formed by Sir Robert Peel in 1829. But the working classes did not trust the police: they believed that they had been purposely set up to suppress rather than protect them. The first two policemen to die on duty were killed in Camden a year later.

On 28 June 1830 the Somers Town neighbourhood was 'thrown into an extraordinary state of agitation' by news of what was described as the 'savage murder' of PC Joseph Grantham. Around 7 p.m., Grantham was called to Thornley Place, Skinner Street, because of a disturbance. A tall and good-looking young Irish bricklayer, Michael Duffey – variously called 'Michael Gavin' or 'Michael Duggan' by different reporters – had just completed his apprenticeship, and had taken several drinks to celebrate. When he returned to his lodgings at No. 15 Thornley Place, he was rather the worse for wear. James Mitchell, another labourer, suggested he sleep it off, but Duffey was spoiling for a fight and struck Mitchell on the cheek. After this he allowed himself to be put to bed, but was woken up when the landlady came home tipsy. Duffey's response to this was to jump out of his ground-floor window – unfortunately landing at the feet of PC Grantham. Grantham told the young Irishman to behave himself or he'd take him to the watch house. But Duffey was still drunk, and when Mitchell came out to see what the noise was about Duffey charged at Mitchell's wife 'like a bullock' and knocked her down. Grantham tried to handcuff the young Irishman, but he resisted. At this point PC William Bennett arrived to help his colleague. But Duffey, using a 'very coarse expression', said he wouldn't be taken by any policeman. After a struggle, Bennett managed to handcuff the prisoner. As Grantham tried to secure Duffey's feet, he was violently kicked in the stomach and the throat. He collapsed, apparently into a fit, and was dead within ten minutes. It was later revealed that the policeman had been financially supporting his elderly mother – and that the day before his murder, PC Grantham's wife had given birth to twins.

At the coroner's inquest, after two doctors gave evidence that Grantham died from apoplexy (a stroke), the jury returned a verdict, 'That the deceased died from extravasation [sic] of blood on the brain, caused by over-excitement in the execution of his duty.' Duffey couldn't be charged with wilful murder, but he was brought before the Middlesex Sessions on 10 July on assault charges. He was found guilty and sentenced to six months in prison for the attack on PC Grantham, and a further six weeks for assaulting PC Bennett.

A second policeman was murdered on duty just six weeks later. On 16 August 1830, soon after midnight, PC John Long was following three men acting suspiciously near King's Cross. He told a colleague that he believed they were casing houses for burglary; tools used for housebreaking were later found abandoned nearby. Catching up with the suspects in Gray's Inn Road, the policeman issued a challenge: 'What have you been after?' The suspects clustered round him, and one man stabbed PC Long with a pointed shoe-maker's knife, thrusting with such force that the blade snapped off in his body. He and a companion ran off down Gray's Inn Road while the third man took off down nearby Wells Street. PC Long fell to the ground, exclaiming, 'Oh God! I am a dead man!' He died before anyone could carry him to a doctor. The fatal knife-blow had gone between his ribs and entered his heart. Long was thirty-six years old.

An arrest was quickly made, but it took nearly a month to establish the accused's identity. He persisted in the lie that he was John Smith, but his real name eventually proved to be William Sapwell. Several witnesses came forward to say he was a baker by trade, including one James Long (no relation to the dead policeman), who revealed Sapwell's

The murder of PC Long in 1830, from the New Newgate Calendar.

criminal past. Sapwell had persuaded Long to help him rob his aunt, then turned informer. As a result of Sapwell's evidence, Long was sentenced to hang (a sentence then commuted to ten years in prison). More recently, Sapwell had served time for running a brothel in Drummond Crescent, St Pancras. Several passers-by swore he had struck the fatal blow, among them Mary Ann Griffiths. That night, she'd been in the pub with a gentleman client – she clearly wasn't the ideal witness. But she had spoken to PC Long earlier that evening, when he'd given her a penny. Under cross-examination, she described herself as an 'unfortunate female, but quite sober on the night of the murder' and maintained she'd clearly seen Sapwell's face as he ran past. Another witness had pursued and identified Sapwell as the killer: 'there was no other person between us,' he said. A watchman – hearing the cry of, 'Stop, Thief! Murder!' – grabbed and detained Sapwell as he passed.

Sapwell protested his innocence. He said that on the evening of the murder he was at the Bedford Tea Gardens in Camden Town, playing skittles until 11 p.m. 'I then walked home and saw a man (PC Long) in pursuit of three others in Gray's Inn Road, but I wasn't involved in the chase or the stabbing.'

No character witnesses came forward to confirm his story, and the jury returned a guilty verdict. Sapwell was sentenced to hang on 20 September.

His execution attracted a larger than usual crowd, with spectators at every window and vantage point overlooking the scaffold. Sapwell asked the officials not to delay: 'Gentlemen, let me not detain you, I am quite ready.' But he maintained his innocence to the end, claiming that when he came before God and was asked what crime he had committed, 'God will shake his head and say, "They sent you wrongfully!"'

AD 1845

DANCING ON THE DEAD

The Enon Chapel Scandal

BY THE NINETEENTH CENTURY many London churchyards were located in the midst of crowded neighbourhoods occupied by poor tenants, who had little or no choice over where they lived. This was an unhealthy situation: decaying and often shallow-buried corpses were a health hazard, polluting water supplies and giving off poisonous gases.

Conditions in and around the Enon Baptist Chapel in Clement's Lane, Holborn, were amongst the very worst. It stood by the entrance to Clement's Inn, in the corner of a dingy court. The site is now covered by the London School of Economics. It was opened in 1822 as a business speculation by Mr Howse, who was both the owner and minister at the chapel. The upper part was used for worship. It was separated by a wooden floor from the vault below, where the first burial took place on 6 October 1822. The vault was well used, especially by the poor, because fees were low: Howse charged eight shillings for a five-year-old child, rising to a maximum of twelve or fifteen shillings per adult, including the service. As many as nine or ten funerals took place on a single Sunday afternoon,

and in the first six years Howse earned £950 (equivalent to £64,000 today).

The congregation, and the children attending Sunday school, sat above these putrid, decaying bodies. The smell was so overpowering that people fainted during the services, especially in hot weather, when insects the locals called 'body bugs' infested the chapel.

Nor was Howse very scrupulous about how he buried his customers, or what happened to their bodies after interment. The Enon vault measured just 60ft by 30ft, with less than 5ft of headroom. Calculations suggested that there was room for 1,200 bodies inside – yet over the space of sixteen years, Howse had supposedly crammed between 10,000 and 12,000 corpses into the space. How was it done? When questioned, a member of the congregation believed that 'a great many [of the bodies] have been removed to make room for others. They used to burn the coffins.' And what happened to the contents? 'I do not know, unless they were shovelled all together, which I believe to be the case in this place.'

It was rumoured that Howse had dropped whole or partially decomposed corpses into a sewer below the vault; others were sold, some for dissection; on others, quicklime was used to speed up decay. When the sewer was repaired, about sixty cartloads of 'rubbish' were moved from the vault and dumped near Waterloo Bridge: 'This consisted partly of earth, of bones and animal matter, and fragments of broken-up or decayed coffins.' The carter gave some earth to men mending the road outside – but when they tipped it up, a human hand fell out: 'It did not appear to have been buried probably a month; it was as near perfect as my hand.'

Howse died in about 1837, and burials ceased. In 1842, the government convened a Select Committee enquiring into the effect of urban burials on the health of the population. But officials were unable to gain access to the Enon vault, concluding 'there must be a very great body of injurious matter kept concealed.' They were quite right. The chapel was no longer a place of worship, but nothing had been done to clear the vault. It remained choked with bodies.

The building went through a brief phase as a Temperance Chapel but, by 1845, and with the vault still stuffed to the rafters with coffins, it had become a dancing saloon. The owners exploited the building's former use, advertising: 'Enon Chapel – Dancing on the Dead. Admission, 3d. No lady or gentleman admitted unless wearing shoes and stockings.'

These entertainments were still taking place several nights a week, when, on 25 October 1847, the chapel was visited by members of the Society for Abolishing Burials in Towns and Cities. This time they were made welcome by the Trustees, who agreed the vaults

were in a frightful state. Further, they would welcome the removal of the human remains but couldn't afford the expense. The men cautiously ventured down into the vault, to find they were standing on engraved coffin plates, with clearly readable inscriptions, which littered the floor. On all sides lay human remains; broken coffins, and other emblems of decayed mortality, scattered in confused heaps. There were several coffins in which lay half-decomposed carcasses, and in the centre was a deep trench, the sides and ends of which were formed by coffins closely packed together. There was a blind window here too. In former days, it was asserted, dead bodies were shot through here and into another cellar (under the minister's house), where they were chopped up and disposed of so as to make room for fresh interments.

This gave substance to the rumours that body parts had been sold. There were also suspiciously high numbers of empty coffins in the vault. On the following Wednesday the vault was opened for the first time to the public – and a huge and eager crowd came to view the gruesome remains.

The problem was solved at last when Mr George Alfred Walker bought the chapel. He was a Drury Lane surgeon who had been instrumental in bringing the dreadful conditions at Enon Chapel to the public's attention. He paid £100 for the human remains to be exhumed and reburied in a single grave, 12ft square by 20ft deep, in West Norwood Cemetery (present whereabouts unknown). The chapel floor was re-laid, and the showman George Sanger took over the building shortly before Christmas 1850.

He staged a pantomime, *Harlequin and the Mountain Snow*, but only stayed a few weeks. His reason for leaving? The fact that the men who'd been hired by Walker to remove the contents of the vault had not completed the job, but had left barrels of remains – and Howse's own coffin – under the new cement floor. A good story, but almost certainly untrue.

Clare Market Chapel, formerly Enon Chapel.

In 1859 the refurbished building opened as Clare Market Chapel, doubling as a school and place of worship. It was demolished when the Carey Street bankruptcy courts were built in the 1890s.

THE MAN IN THE LONG BLACK CLOAK

The True Story of the Delarue Murder

ON FRIDAY EVENING, 21 February 1845, Edward Hilton, a baker from West End (today's West Hampstead), was making his last delivery in Haverstock Terrace. He was shocked to hear cries of 'murder' from the open fields beyond the houses. It was about 7 p.m. on a misty moonlit night. He couldn't see anything, but he reported the incident to PC John Baldock, who was on patrol. Baldock met up with Sergeant Thomas Fletcher and together they searched the fields between Haverstock Hill and Finchley Road. Near a stile by the wall of Belsize House they discovered the body of a well-dressed young man lying on his back in a pool of blood.

Fletcher left Baldock guarding the body while he went to get a stretcher. As he waited, the PC was startled to hear singing and whistling, and was even more surprised when a man in a long black cloak appeared out of the darkness, calling, 'Hello, policeman, what have you got there?' A dead body, the policeman replied. The stranger said, 'Are you quite sure he is dead?' He bent down to feel the pulse – saying, as he did, 'You have got a nasty job alone here.' He waited with Baldock, and even gave him a shilling to get some brandy. After twenty minutes help arrived and the body was taken to the Yorkshire Grey pub in Hampstead. The stranger followed the group for some way before departing.

The man had been killed by six or seven blows to the head with a heavy instrument. No watch or money was found, but there was a letter in his coat pocket from a woman who hinted she was pregnant and asked him to meet her. It was signed 'Caroline'. On Sunday the body was identified as that of twenty-nine-year-old James Delarue, a teacher of music who lodged at No. 55 Whittlebury Street, Euston

West End in around 1840, by Fancourt. (T. J. Barratt, Annals of Hampstead, *1912)*

Square, and who had been missing since Friday evening.

The news of the Hampstead murder swept through London. William Watson, landlord of No. 17 Charles Street, became suspicious when he discovered that his lodgers, Mr and Mrs Hocker, had received money from their son Tom, who'd been a good friend of Delarue. Watson had also seen Hocker on Saturday night with money and new clothes. He told the police. After searching the house, they arrested twenty-one-year-old Thomas Henry Hocker. Like the victim, Hocker earned his living by occasionally teaching music, reading and writing to private families.

In court, Thomas's younger brother, James, gave evidence. He said he lived with his father, a ladies' shoemaker, at 17 Charles Street, Portland Town (St John's Wood); however, because there was not enough room at No. 17, he and his brother slept across the road at No. 11 Victoria Terrace. James said that Tom was a good friend of Delarue and, because he was not in regular employment, Delarue would give Tom money. On the day of the murder, Tom told his family he was going to collect a loan of ten or twelve sovereigns from a Mrs Edwards. When the police interviewed the lady, however, she said she hadn't lent Hocker any money.

Other evidence was brought forward. The police found blood-stained clothes and a total of seventy-six letters, all in women's handwriting, in Hocker's lodgings. There was also an exact copy of the 'Caroline' letter found in the murdered man's pocket. Two silk buttons were missing from Hocker's overcoat,

A contemporary sketch showing the finding of the victim in the Delarue murder. (Lloyd's Penny Sunday Times, *16 March 1845*)

and matching buttons were found at the scene of the murder. A search of the cesspools at Charles Street produced a diamond ring, which Daniel Delarue said belonged to his murdered brother. Police also found his missing gold watch chain, covered with blood stains. In Delarue's apartment they discovered a number of obscene books and prints. It was clear that Delarue and Hocker were 'young bucks' who had lied to and misled a large number of young women.

Thousands of people visited the murder site, despite the field having been covered in a thick layer of manure to renovate the down-trodden grass; 'Hundreds of the fairer sex were to be seen wending their way up to their ankles in mire, to gratify their morbid curiosity.' Souvenir-hunters removed pieces of the stile Delarue was supposed to have been crossing when he was killed, and bricks from the wall. The murdered man was buried in Hampstead churchyard on 2 March.

At his trial, Hocker smiled frequently during the evidence given by witnesses and took pinches of snuff. He read out two statements he'd prepared which attempted to explain his bloody clothes. Both were bizarre. Hocker admitted he'd

Thomas Henry Hocker. (Pictorial Times, 29 March 1845)

at 7 p.m., he had heard the cry of 'murder' coming from the spot where the brother had met Delarue. Because he held himself responsible for the tragedy, he decided to take on all the blame. He therefore visited a slaughterhouse to get his clothes bloody, to add further weight to his story.

The jury didn't believe Hocker, and took ten minutes to convict him. He was hanged at Newgate on 28 April 1845, in front of a large crowd, just before his twenty-second birthday.

The following year Charles Dickens wrote a letter to the *Daily News*, printed on 9 March 1846. Dickens believed that Hocker carefully planned the murder as a means of gaining fame and notoriety. It had all the elements of melodrama:

known Delarue for nearly two years. He further admitted that he had been the man who'd waited beside the body with PC Baldock. Hocker then told an elaborate story to explain the murder, based on the unknown 'Caroline'. He said he'd courted a young lady in Hampstead for about a year. He and Delarue frequently visited her family, but Delarue betrayed him and became the woman's lover. Hocker said he wrote the letter found in Delarue's pocket, using a disguised hand, as part of a plan to get Delarue to meet Caroline's brother (not named) in the fields behind Haverstock Hill. Hocker then suggested that the brother had killed Delarue because he had got his sister pregnant.

Hocker insisted that he had waited in the Swiss Tavern (at Swiss Cottage) whilst the brother committed the crime;

> Here is an insolent, flippant, dissolute youth: aping the man of intrigue and levity: over-dressed, over-confident, inordinately vain of his personal appearance ... and unhappily the son of a working shoemaker. Bent on loftier flights ... and having no truth, industry, perseverance, or other dull work-a-day quality, to plume his wings withal; he casts about him, in his jaunty way, for some mode of distinguishing himself... of making the life and adventures of Thomas Hocker remarkable...
>
> A murder, now, would make a noise in the papers! There is the gallows to be sure; but without that, it would be nothing. Short of that, it wouldn't be fame. Well! We must all die at one time or other; and to die game, and have it in print, is just the thing for a man of spirit.

AD 1857

THE CAMDEN TOWN STAMPEDE!

THE *MORNING CHRONICLE* described the 'extraordinary and horrifying scene' at the Camden Town warehouse of Pickfords the carriers after its destruction by fire on 9 June 1857: 'There has been no fire in the metropolis, which for its intensity, illuminating power, or annihilation of valuable property, has exceeded that at the Camden-station.'

It was shortly after 10 p.m. that the cry of 'fire' first rang through the building. Camden Town was an important reception and dispatch centre, providing Pickfords with access to the Regent's Canal and the tracks of the London and North Western Railway (LNWR). Their lines ran across the canal into the warehouse. There had been an unusual number of late business transactions, and clerks were hard at work on invoices when the fire began. The flames spread so rapidly that many of the terrified office workers had to run for their lives.

The blaze was first spotted in the stores where hay and fodder were kept. This was a horse-drawn society, and Pickfords kept a large number to pull their carts and wagons. Around 150 employees tried to extinguish the flames, but in

less than five minutes the hay store was consumed. The fire spread to the stables in vaults below the warehouse – where 100 horses were in danger of being burned to death. Dense and suffocating smoke filled the building and spilt into the surrounding streets. The heat caused gin casks to burst (though, unlike the experience of Langdale's Distillery during the Gordon Riots, no one tried to collect the spirits). Instead, the gin flowed, like a sheet of liquid fire, into the stables below. Brave volunteers joined Pickfords' staff to release the horses.

The terrified horses stampeded down Oval Road into the streets of Camden Town. Many were driven towards Highgate, where they almost overran Police Inspector Fidge on his way to fight the fire. He was severely shocked but unhurt. Poultry, goats and pigs perished in the flames, but only one bad-tempered horse – known as 'the man-hater' – died. In the absence of his keeper, he lived up to his name and bit anyone who tried to lead him out. 'The shouts of the people, the furious raging of the fire, the screaming whistles of the railway engines, the cracking of the ignited timber and continuous

Right *Contemporary engraving showing the horses stampeding.*

Below *Crowds on Primrose Hill watching the Camden Town fire.*

explosions of combustibles within the building, all contributed to produce an effect which may be better imagined than described.'

'Wagon after wagon and truck load upon truck load of goods dropped down with a loud crash,' wrote a contemporary source, when, at around 11.30 p.m., the floor above the stables collapsed. The entire north wall fell into the canal, on top of two barges, partially blocking the waterway. The water for the fire fighters didn't flow as it should,

even though the canal was used. All the crews of the several fire engines could do was to confine the blaze to Pickfords' building and concentrate on saving neighbouring properties.

At one point the flames were higher than the roof of the Stanhope Arms immediately opposite Pickfords' gates. George Freeborn, the landlord, was distraught. One engine pumped water onto the front of the building, but the walls were so hot it turned into clouds of steam. Finally, thanks to the efforts of the firemen, the pub survived, as did the nearby Camden Flour Mills, the premises of salt merchant Henry Munday and Collard's piano factory, immediately south of the blaze.

About an acre of Pickfords' premises was reduced to rubble. Given the widespread destruction, it was a miracle no one was killed. In the clerks' quarters the company safe remained suspended on brickwork, but the bottom had burned out, destroying any valuables, cash or papers. Thousands of people came to view the smouldering ruins and many tried to secure souvenirs.

Among the more bizarre claims, it was reported that Professor Anderson, the 'Wizard of the North', had lost his 'stupendously magnificent paraphernalia' valued at £7,000. John Henry Anderson was a blacksmith who became a great magician and illusionist, and was supposed to be the first man ever to pull a rabbit out of a hat. Anderson was opening at the Standard Theatre in London's Shoreditch on the 15th and the fire gave him the perfect opportunity to publicise the 'miraculous escape' of his equipment, which was fortunately on a train that hadn't arrived at Camden Town. As Anderson had been almost twice bankrupted by theatre fires, the ultimate irony would have been if his new props had burned.

Mr Huish, general manager of the LNWR, informed the press in the week following the fire that reports had greatly exaggerated the value of the goods destroyed: figures of £250,000 were circulating. The true figure, including buildings, was likely to be around a quarter of that sum. Fortunately, the warehouse had been relatively empty, as most trains had already departed, and the building was well insured – as were the goods inside. 'I may add that the business has not been interrupted,' he added. Temporary premises had been opened the day after the fire, alongside the canal. Many newspapers claimed the clerks had fled, leaving their account books open on their desks. This was contradicted by Pickfords' employees, who wrote that most of the records had been saved, the staff working until they too were in danger of being engulfed by the flames.

On the night of the fire the surrounding streets were crammed with spectators, while even more crowded nearby vantage points, including Primrose Hill. The blaze lit up the night sky for miles around and firemen were still damping down the ruins the following evening. When Pickfords' premises were rebuilt, their footprint was enlarged: an extra storey was added and the vaults were converted into stores. New stables were provided off site in Gloucester Avenue, reached by a tunnel under the railway lines.

THE KENTISH TOWN CATASTROPHE

The Railway Crash of 1861

ON THE EVENING of Monday, 2 September 1861, at around 7.15 p.m., an excursion train from Kew hit an empty ballast train on a bridge about 450 yards south of today's Gospel Oak station (London Overground). The station was then called Kentish Town. The crash occurred roughly where the tracks intersected Carker's Lane, the line running on an embankment some 30ft above ground level. Today this is just a short cul-de-sac, but in 1861 the lane ran westwards from Highgate Road, across open fields to Gospel Oak.

Nineteen-year-old Henry Rayner, a porter at the station, had been a railway employee for only eight months. However, he was regularly left to manage traffic and signalling on his own. On this fateful evening he allowed the passenger train through without making sure that the line was clear. In the crash, the excursion train's engine and three carriages fell on one side of the embankment, and trucks from the ballast train on the other. An onlooker said the steam rushed out of the damaged engine with enough force to destroy haystacks 200 yards away.

Terrified passengers who had escaped the wreck fled across the fields to safety. All evening, sightseers crowded the crash site, where a carriage was set on fire to provide light for the rescuers, revealing an awful sight: 'The wounded lay here and there, writhing in agony. Men were engaged in dragging corpses from under wheels and out of carriages that had been crushed like pasteboard. The bodies of four or five of the dead were completely flattened.'

Of the 500 passengers, sixteen died and over 300 were injured, twenty seriously. Most were railway employees, their friends and families. Ironically, they were on a fund-raising trip held for

The awful scene at the accident.

the benefit of colleagues who suffered accidents at work.

The wreckage was removed during the following Saturday night, disappointing the enormous crowds that again turned up on Sunday. The police were called in to clear the site, under the direction of Inspector Fitch (who had also been involved with the investigation of the Pickfords' fire in 1857). Traders seized upon an opportunity to make money: 'Throughout the day the Kentish Town fields were like a fair, and vendors of fruit and sweetmeats reaped a plentiful harvest.' Prayers were said for the victims in local churches and open-air services were held. Today the railway is hemmed in on both sides by trading estates or houses, and the span at the end of Arctic Street provides the closest public access to the crash site.

The inquest was held at the Vestry Hall (equivalent to today's Town Hall). The jury visited the site at Kentish Town; they also had the gruesome task of viewing the bodies of the deceased. Some of the descriptions show how violent the collision had been. James English, a French polisher, had been travelling with his wife when the accident occurred. He survived, but the 'mangled remains' of Emma English were 'such as to appal the stoutest heart'. Seven bodies at University College Hospital presented such a dreadful sight that 'several of the (jury) rushed out of the room after the first glance. The imagination could conceive no idea of the fractures, the lacerations, and the disfigurements of most of those corpses.'

Among the dead was the fireman of the excursion train, twenty-two-year-old George Bolton, who ended up under the engine. He crawled out, his

The jury viewing the scene of the Kentish Town railway disaster.

clothes on fire, and died of his burns a few days later.

Considering the carriages were wood and flimsily constructed, some people had miraculous escapes. James Newcombe, along with forty-nine others, was in the first carriage, which was described as being 'smashed to atoms'. He talked of being tossed about, 'horribly entangled with his fellow passengers', but when the carriage hit the ground a panel dislodged and he was thrown out. He walked away, bruised but otherwise unhurt. The driver of the excursion train, George Scott, fell down the embankment among the ballast trucks, but survived with burns and a broken arm. The guard, Joseph Brydges, also broke his arm and was concussed; he was in a brake van that fell into the road below the bridge.

Other stories were heart-breaking. There was a baby girl, aged around eight months, who was healthy but unclaimed by any survivor. Mr George Greenwood wept as he told the inquest of identifying the bodies of his two sons, Charles, aged eleven, and Henry, seven, who had died of internal injuries. His wife Jane was

1867: MAN ATTACKED BY CAT

In this decade, in June 1867, George Amey was charged with attacking his estranged wife Isabella Amey, who lived at 36 Tottenham Street. He knocked her down, jumped on her and tried to strangle her. Help came from an unexpected quarter: Isabella's cat Topsy sprang at George. It fastened its claws in George's eyes and bit his face. The cat wouldn't let go, and eventually George had to beg Isabella for help. He was sent to prison for a month for assault.

considered too ill to be told the truth. Charles Cox, a railway signalman, had been on a day trip with his wife Sarah. He gave evidence from his hospital bed concerning the signal lights. It was a truly melancholy sight to witness his sufferings. Reports said how he breathed as if a hydraulic press was being applied to bring his chest and back together. The sweat rolled in large drops from his head and face. Several times there was a long and painful pause, during which Cox convulsively grasped a handle suspended from the ceiling for the purpose of enabling him to change his position. His wife was less severely injured, but Charles died a few weeks later.

The Official Enquiry said that it was almost certain the accident would not have happened if the railway company had set up proper signals, to regulate the ballast train traffic to and from sidings under construction. Contributory causes included a steep curve that restricted the train driver's view and the fact the excursion train had arrived earlier than expected. Although the inquest criticised the railway company for using inexperienced staff, it concluded Rayner was responsible for causing the accident and he was committed for trial for manslaughter. Perhaps anticipating the outcome, he left the inquest before the verdict. Surprisingly, however, Rayner was acquitted that October on a legal technicality. He remained in railway employment for the rest of his life, as a clerk.

The following year, two passengers won compensation. William Read, a plasterer from Bow, was in the second carriage. The impact trapped him by the legs but he managed to free himself and rescue his wife and child from the wreckage. 'My eye was nearly cut out, and I had a pain in my shoulder for six weeks, and could not follow my trade. I am, even now, far from being the man I was, nor can I do the work I did before the accident.' He was awarded £500. James English, husband of poor Emma English, was awarded £1,000 for his own injuries with £200 to his seven children 'for the loss of their mother's services.'

AD 1866

'HUMAN JAM'

St Giles and St Pancras Burial Grounds

ST PANCRAS GARDENS on Pancras Road opened in 1877. This public open space was originally two burial grounds belonging to the parishes of St Pancras and St Giles, Holborn. The southern part was dedicated to St Pancras, embracing the original parish church. The St Giles graveyard opened in 1803 and lay north of the church, behind the present St Pancras Hospital and what was then St Pancras workhouse, home for the destitute. Many eminent people were buried here, alongside ordinary Londoners, local residents and paupers.

As the capital grew, parishes such as St Giles were forced to purchase land some distance away for burials. But by the mid-nineteenth century, conditions in the relatively new St Giles' ground were among the worst in London. 'In an acre in the immediate vicinity of St Pancras Workhouse, between 1843 and 1845, no fewer than 10,000 bodies were interred in this space alone.' At least another 3,000 were buried during the subsequent cholera epidemic. The graves were so close to the workhouse that the smell was dreadful, with 'offensive matter percolating through the walls into the sleeping apartments.' And it got worse...

In 1846 work was begun on expanding St Giles' own workhouse off Endell Street, Holborn, taking in most of the adjacent paupers' graveyard. What happened next was likened to the scandal of Enon Chapel. The public was alerted when bones and a couple of skulls were found dumped near King's Cross. This forced the parish authorities to exhume all the bodies and re-bury them in their Pancras Road ground. But that October a horrific report appeared, describing conditions at the Holborn site. There were so many corpses, it said, sometimes fourteen in one grave, that large wooden boxes had been hastily ordered, the bodies piled into them for transportation and reburial. Some were found to be in a remarkable state of preservation, 'the hair upon the eyebrows and eyelashes clearly discernible, and every feature entire.' It was planned to spread concrete over any remaining graves.

An 1849 inspection at Pancras Road revealed three open pits in the St Giles section, containing piles of coffins. 'The most offensive emanations were passing off from those pits of corruption, which were extremely injurious to the poor inmates of the workhouse... It was stated that a body had been chopped up to make room for others, and that it was so fresh that its blood bespattered the workhouse wall.'

In 1848, the adjacent old parish church of St Pancras had been partially rebuilt, which work took in part of that parish's burial ground. R.L. Roumieu, one of the architects, described the clay as being 'so saturated with decomposition as to be horribly foetid. The ordinary excavators were made sick, although frequently given spirits by the contractors to prevent nausea; and their place was taken by some seasoned gravediggers.' No less than 26,676 burials were recorded in the St Pancras section alone between 1827 and 1847.

In 1854, both the St Giles' and St Pancras' grounds were closed for burials, but the dead were not allowed to rest in peace. The Midland Railway was given permission to tunnel 12ft beneath, and to build across a section of the cemetery, en route to its St Pancras' terminus. The work began in 1866 with the demolition of hundreds of properties. It was reported that the workhouse was

Two different views of St Pancras' church, before and after the rebuild, showing the work in action.

crammed to bursting point, as there was no obligation to re-house anyone who'd lost their home. 'The railway is no respecter of persons, living or dead. Trains will be constantly flying past the very windows of the church, and be rumbling over the tombs of the hallowed dead.'

The first graves were opened when a temporary viaduct was built. The smell was dreadful. Human remains were scattered across the excavations while the vicar complained of 'dead men's shanks and yellow skulls, packed higgledy-piggledy into a large wooden box, and when one coffin was stove in by a blow of a spade, a fair, bright tress of hair was seen.' Many joined with the vicar in protesting the 'desecration' of the site, and 'the coarse language and oaths of the labourers.' It was predicted the tunnelling would reveal fresh horrors. Roumieu said pits packed with paupers' coffins would be disturbed: 'being full of water, you may imagine the pleasant dropping which will take place through the very pervious arching which forms the roofs of most tunnels, when this reservoir of decomposition overlies the top of it.' A distance of 12ft was considered a safe depth, but the excavators immediately encountered human remains. That November, the vicar of old St Pancras' reported 700 bodies had been removed.

The protests ensured that work stopped until a piece of ground behind the St Pancras workhouse was consecrated. A pit 40ft deep was dug for reburial (at the Midland's expense) of the exhumed remains. How many bodies were reinterred is impossible to say, for in many cases all that survived were quantities of loose bones and skulls.

The architect Arthur Blomfield was appointed as supervisor, and in turn sent one of his young assistants, twenty-six-year-old Thomas Hardy, to check all was done correctly. It was ghastly work.

After nightfall, within a high hoarding, and by the light of flare-lamps, the exhumation went on continuously of the coffins that had been uncovered during the day, new coffins being provided for those that had come apart and for loose skeletons.

Reburials continued until March 1867. It had a profound effect on Hardy: in his poem *The Levelled Churchyard* he wrote:

We late-lamented resting here, are mixed to human jam
And each to each exclaims in fear, I know not which I am!

Today, the Hardy Tree stands behind the old church, surrounded by 496 tombstones rescued by Thomas. The monument to writers William Godwin and his wife Mary (better known as Wollstonecraft) was destroyed, but their bodies had been removed in 1851. Their daughter Mary married Percy Bysshe Shelley after secret lovers' trysts in the graveyard.

In 2002, history repeated itself: 2,000 more bodies had to be exhumed to build the Channel Tunnel rail link. Once more the headline 'graves desecrated' alerted the public, as mechanical diggers scraped bodies up from the ground and dumped bones in bags for reburial. Work was suspended until archaeologists, who had been banned from the site, were able to resume work alongside specialist contractors.

AD 1867

SKATING ON THIN ICE

The Regent's Park Disaster

HEAVY SNOW BLANKETED London during the first weeks of January 1867. The 14th was bitterly cold, and temperatures barely made it above freezing all day. The lake in Regent's Park was thronged with thousands of skaters and sliders, but by late afternoon numbers had dwindled to a few hundred. The centre of activity was the ice, between islands, in front of Hanover Gate. Spectators lined the shore to watch friends and family, and enterprising salesmen hired skates to eager customers. But the condition of the ice wasn't good. Experienced employees of the Royal Humane Society (RHS), known as 'icemen', repeatedly warned of the danger.

Disaster struck soon after 4 p.m.: the ice collapsed, plunging about 200 skaters into the lake, which was 12ft deep in places, with a thick layer of mud on the bottom.

The terrified skaters thrashed about in the freezing water, weighed down by their clothes and skates. Within minutes, around 100 people had struggled to the shore or to one of the islands, while others lay flat or clung to pieces of ice. Some became chilled and let go, with 'the most piteous calls for help and then sinking with dismal wailings to their death'. A joined-up rope was stretched from shore to shore, and a few skaters managed to grab it. The RHS had a couple of wicker boats, and other pleasure craft were launched, but it was hard to push them through the broken ice. Iceman Alfred Ward had earlier warned skaters, in no uncertain terms, to leave: 'For God Almighty's sake go off, or there will be a general calamity before long.' He saved seven people; William Archer, manager of the pleasure boats,

The awful moment when the ice cracked!

was later awarded a medal for rescuing a further nine skaters.

It was in the middle of the lake that the tragedy played out, where rescue ladders were useless and the broken, lumpy ice hindered the passage of any boat. Women rushed about on the banks screaming out that their children, husbands or brothers were drowning, and imploring the bystanders to save them. Boys and girls stood hysterically crying and wringing their hands, and between their sobs exclaiming, 'Oh, look at father!'

Once enough ice had been cleared, the grim task of recovering the bodies of those who had drowned could begin. It went on for several days, during which 'all that remained was floating hats and sticks'.

There were, however, some lucky escapes. Frederick Dunton was making his way to the bank with his eleven-year-old son Frank and seven-year-old daughter when the ice broke. He watched his children sink out of sight – but then, mercifully, they bobbed up again and he grabbed them with one hand, holding onto the ice with the other; 'Heads and arms were all around amongst the broken masses of ice. Two yards away from me a little boy was drowning, and I could not render him any help,' he later reported. Dunton stood for fully half an hour, in 5ft of water, slowly sinking into the mud. In desperation, he told young Frank to wave his walking stick. They were rescued by William Archer, who swam out: he lifted the girl onto his back and took her to his boat before returning for Frank and Dunton, who reached the shore hanging onto the side. Although no official was criticised for dereliction of

Dragging the Regent's Park lake for the bodies.

duty, Dunton maintained that one of the RHS's men refused to help them, telling onlookers, 'he could do no good for us.'

Sixteen-year-old Frederick Selous showed great presence of mind. He was on the ice and watched in horror as skaters some distance from the shore disappeared under slabs of ice which immediately closed over them. He lay down on a large piece and cautiously crawled from one slab to another until he reached an island, and from there the shore. Selous went on to become a renowned hunter and explorer.

Another survivor was nicknamed 'the man with the pipe'. George Pinkerton clung to a block of ice, calmly smoking his pipe while others round him were picked up. Then, suddenly realising the danger he was in, he cried: '£50 to anyone who will fetch me out!' Several attempts were made before George Matthews (who couldn't swim) stripped to his shirt and trousers and, with a rope round his waist, fought his way through the ice and seized the skater. To loud cheers, both were pulled to shore. The skater later wrote to *The Times* denying he'd offered any reward, and chose to sign his letter, 'The man with the pipe'.

It transpired that no one had the funds or the authority to co-ordinate the subsequent search-and-recovery operation. The master of nearby Marylebone workhouse took it upon himself to make the workhouse facilities available to the injured, dying and dead: cab drivers only agreed to take rescued skaters home after a local resident volunteered to pay their fares. The rescue equipment belonging to the RHS – a voluntary organisation – was woefully inadequate to the task. In the days that followed, the ice had to be removed daily to provide clear water for boats and divers. By Saturday, cash had to be raised to continue the clearance, starting with a collection among bystanders. The divers were free, and were supplied by the inventor of the diving suit, Mr Heinke. It also emerged that no one had the right to order people off the ice – not park officials, the RHS or the police.

A total of forty skaters died, making this the worst ice accident in the UK's history. There were no women among the dead, most of whom were men from Marylebone, Islington, Camden and Kentish Towns. The youngest was Charles Jukes, age nine; the oldest was forty. Nearly half were under twenty. A black retriever dog, thought to belong to one of the dead, remained by the lake for several days, in great distress and refusing all attempts to feed him.

The inquest concluded that the accident had happened because too many people were on thin and partially thawed ice that couldn't support them. The fact that the lake was so deep

Divers searching for bodies in Regent's Park lake.

contributed to the number of fatalities, and it was recommended it be reduced to 4ft or 5ft, which was done. No mention was made of the long-standing practice of breaking the ice away from the shore to prevent skaters landing on the private gardens fringing the lake. Several persons had alleged that this probably weakened the ice. Selous always believed this caused the accident. The father of Charles Jukes said servants from private houses took water from the lake, breaking ice at the edge, and he cried out as he left the inquest, 'I call it murder'. But some newspapers criticised the skaters for being reckless: 'the death they met with was the result of their excessive foolhardiness in remaining upon the ice to steal a few extra moment's enjoyment at a fearful risk.' They called it 'suicide by skating'.

History repeated itself in 1886. On 9 January, skaters ignored warning signs and took to the ice. An estimated 100 people were on the ice when it collapsed. This time no lives were lost, however, largely because the water level had been lowered.

AD 1874

THE AMAZING TRUE STORY OF 'BLOW UP' BRIDGE!

IT WAS SHORTLY before 5 a.m. on Friday, 2 October 1874 when Henry Coysh went off duty and walked through the rain to his home in Charles Street. He was the night-time gatekeeper of the Macclesfield Bridge over the Regent's Canal, at the southern end of Avenue Road. A few minutes later the neighbourhood was rocked by a massive explosion immediately under the bridge, and a column of fire lit up the sky. Rubble rained down on the neighbouring streets and houses of Primrose Hill and St John's Wood, and windows were shattered along the Edgware Road, Regent's Park Road and Camden High Street. Coysh had a miraculous escape, although many properties in his street were damaged. The enormous sound, and the impact of the shockwave, were reported as far away as Enfield, Blackheath, Norwood and Bayswater and caused panic among local residents. Some thought there had been an earthquake; others believed that the Fenians (Irish independence fighters) were responsible. Some even believed that Judgement Day had arrived. A doctor living alongside Primrose Hill described the moment the blast hit: 'Men, women and children rushing about in a state of semi-nudity, uttering the most hideous cries. One lady in her nightdress clung to me exclaiming, "Is it come? Is it come?"'

Another person wrote, 'At first we thought it was the end of days, the crack of doom. The fright, the horror, in the dead of night, all terrified nearly to death, some screaming, some fainting...'

But there had been no divine intervention. At around 3 a.m., a steam tug had left the City Road canal basin towing five boats owned by the Grand Junction Canal Company: the *Jane*, the *Dee*, the *Tilbury*, the *Limehouse* and the *Hawkesbury*. Their mixed cargo included coffee, sugar and rice, but the middle boat also had benzoline (benzine) and 5 tons of gunpowder on board. Having passed safely through Kentish and Camden Town locks, they continued west towards Paddington. But then, as it passed under Macclesfield Bridge, the *Tilbury* exploded, wrecking the *Limehouse*, the boat immediately behind. Part of the *Tilbury*'s keel fell on a roof 300 yards away, 'passing through three floors to the basement, rebounding again into the parlour.'

The scene after the explosion on the Regent's Canal.

The canal company hired a gang of 100 labourers who worked around the clock to clear the debris from the canal bed, which was dammed with debris.

The novelist Joseph Hatton, who lived close by in Titchfield Terrace, Prince Albert Road, wrote:

> Darkness was made visible by a lurid light that came, with a howling wind, through openings all around us. We were covered in broken glass, hampered with blinds and curtains, blocked in by fallen roofs and doors. Every door and window was blown in. From kitchen to attic the ruin is equally distributed through every apartment.

Given the rain of stones, bricks and shards of glass, it's amazing the only fatalities were the three-man crew of the *Tilbury*. It could have been far, far worse. Most people were still in bed. There weren't many properties immediately south of the canal, which at this point ran in a cutting where the banks deflected the blast. The destruction of the bridge also absorbed some of the explosion. However, the nature and extent of the damage astounded reporters and many thousands came to see for themselves: 'Omnibuses ran full "to the explosion", traffic on the Metropolitan Railway [which then linked Baker Street and Swiss Cottage] became impeded, and it was as much as 500 policemen could do to cope with the oppressive curiosity of the holidaymakers.' The bridge was destroyed, its iron pillars – filled with brick and concrete – snapped in two.

Townsend House, just a few doors away from Joseph Hatton, was also severely damaged. This was the home of artist Alma Tadema, who was visiting Scotland at the time of the accident. However, his children and nanny had stayed behind. 'The children had one consolation. The *Tilbury* was partly laden with nuts which have been blown over Mr Tadema's garden.'

Mr Bartlett, superintendent of the nearby London Zoo, rushed to check for damage, fearing 'the shock might have removed the bolts from the dens of some of the greater carnivores, whose presence at large in the neighbourhood might have been even more fatal to life than the explosion had been.' Happily, all the cages were secure – though the antelopes, giraffes and deer were badly affected, visibly terrified and actually trembling.

One curious incident concerned the gravestone of religious prophetess Joanna Southcott, in the burial ground of St John's Wood church. The stone was shattered by the blast. Her followers hoped this was a sign she was about to return.

The worst damage lay east of the church towards and beyond Primrose Hill, including Portland Town, a network of small streets off Prince Albert Road. This ran along the north side of the canal, where properties 'bore all the appearance of having recently been bombarded. Every window was cracked and shivered; the railings in front were wrenched from the walls, and twisted into the most curious shapes.'

Residents wanted to know if insurance companies would pay for the damage as many policies provided cover for fire but not explosion. Would leasehold tenants have to repair their properties? Local residents, including Joseph Hatton, started a public subscription to help residents who had little money, especially those with businesses to keep going. Over £6,000 was raised, £100 of

which was donated by the gunpowder manufacturers.

What had caused the explosion? Had the gunpowder on board the *Tilbury* been ignited by a lightning strike, sparks from the tug boat or by men smoking nearby? The inquiry revealed bad practice on the part of the Canal Company, allowing a second highly inflammable cargo to be stored close to the gunpowder. The barge was also carrying four barrels of refined benzoline, and it was finally determined that vapour escaping from these casks had run, under a protective tarpaulin, into the cabin, where it was ignited by a small fire for cooking.

Thomas Keates, a consulting chemist, gave evidence at the inquest. 'Supposing the benzoline vapour escaped and reached the cabin, would it travel back alight to the general cargo?' he was asked. Keates replied, 'I am constrained to say that I think this was the cause of the explosion. Distributed as that cargo was, the flame travelling

Maccesfield Bridge, by Thomas Shepard, in 1827.

back would be very likely to ignite the powder. Nothing, in fact, could be more improper than the storage of gunpowder and benzoline together.'

It could have been even worse: the *Dee* was also carrying a barrel of gunpowder, as well as ten of petroleum and two casks of spirits.

It emerged that Tuesdays and Fridays were 'powder' carrying days on the canal. During the following weeks, gunpowder continued to be transported, 80 tons on one day alone. The growing public outcry forced the canal company, reluctantly, to end this practice. It was found guilty, at the inquest that followed, of 'gross negligence', while the existing law was described as 'entirely inadequate'.

In May 1875 local resident Captain Jackson successfully sued for damage to his property. The company accepted the judgement and therefore the liability for damage claims, which in turn resulted in a reduced dividend for shareholders. Macclesfield Bridge reopened in February 1876 after many complaints about its prolonged closure. It is still often referred to by its nickname, 'Blow Up Bridge'.

The Times concluded that, in terms of the area affected, the Regent's Park incident had been 'the most widespread disaster which has occurred in London from explosion in our time'. The disaster brought about some significant changes. On 1 January 1876, a new Act came into force, for the better regulation of the storage, handling and transport of all explosive materials. The Grand Junction Canal Company redesigned their barges for carrying gunpowder and banned mixed cargoes. And, to the relief of many living near the Regent's Canal, the company finally stopped transporting gunpowder through London.

AD 1879

WHO KILLED MATILDA?

The Euston Square Mystery

IT WAS FIFTEEN-YEAR-OLD errand boy Willy Strohman who found the first bones, on the morning of 9 May 1879. He was cleaning out a coal cellar belonging to No. 4 Euston Square, and there 'found a large bone like a person's leg, which came up with the shovel'. He ran for help, and brought two men from nearby businesses, furniture maker Joseph Savage and local coalman George Fulcher. Savage investigated the pile, and found a body there:

> The head was in a corner of the cellar and the legs laid out straight — I laid hold of something; I cannot tell you whether it was cloth or clothing, it came away immediately... [The body] was decomposed to a great extent — there was no smell from it when I first went in...

The corpse was wearing what appeared to be a silk dress. The two men ran for the police, and two constables, Isaac Dowding and Thomas Holman, came to view the body. Fulcher pulled some pieces of clothing from the body, and revealed 'a rope [wrapped] twice round the neck; it had the appearance of a clothes line'.

The policemen put a knife to the rope: 'it was rotten and broke ... the sides of the neck were partly decomposed, but not the front, and there appeared to be the flesh with the clothes line in it.'

A doctor who lived at No. 1 was woken, and came to view the terrible sight. 'On going in from the light,' he said:

> I could see nothing but a black mass, a black mound, but on more closely examining I found at the end of the mound the head of a female — the remains had coal-dust on them, from which they were quite black...

Cellar at 4 Euston Square. (Courtesy of Camden Local Studies and Archive Centre)

69

Matilda Hacker. (Courtesy of Camden Local Studies and Archive Centre)

The doctor directed the remains be taken to St Pancras mortuary, where they were examined in more detail. Over the next few days the cellar was also more thoroughly sifted, and gave up some pieces of jewellery, 'some small human bones, some pieces of female wearing apparel, portions of flesh, and a small bunch of hair with flesh adhering to it... [as well as] a human foot with some signs of leather on it ... some more bones and some wearing apparel.'

The householder at No. 4 was Severin Bastendorff. Born in Luxemburg, the four Bastendorff brothers came to London in the 1870s and set up in business as bamboo furniture makers. In 1876 Severin took a lease of No. 4; there was a workshop in the back garden, ideal for furniture making. (The site now lies under the forecourt of Euston Station.) The family supplemented their income by letting rooms, relying on their servant, Hannah Dobbs, to take care of day-to-day domestic affairs.

The papers were soon full of the ghastly discovery, and Hannah's parents in Bideford began to worry. They feared the corpse was their daughter, as she'd not been in touch for some time. However, their fears were put to rest when the police informed them Hannah was, in fact, in prison, serving an eight-month sentence for theft. But if the body wasn't Hannah's, then whose was it? Medical examination showed it to be that of a woman, aged probably fifty or sixty years old and around 5ft 6in tall. The features had gone; the arms and legs were separated from the trunk, while both hands and one foot had disintegrated. There were curls of pale hair still adhering to the skull and a spinal formation which would have produced a stoop. Given the current state of forensics, no one was able to establish the cause of death. The cord was found to be tightly wrapped around her neck, but whether her death had been caused by hanging or strangulation could never be proved. As for when she died, opinions varied widely – from one to over three years ago.

In common with many London houses, No. 4 had an outside coal cellar – two, in fact. These were under the pavement, with a removable iron plate to allow coal to be poured into the space below. One was used by Bastendorff to store bamboo, and the other, where the body was found, for tenant's coals. This latter cellar was accessed through a scullery inside the house. There were many theories as to how and when the body had arrived in the cellar, but police enquiries soon focused on the obvious conclusion – that the woman had lived at No. 4. A likely candidate soon emerged: Matilda Hacker, an eccentric sixty-six-year-old spinster. She rented a room from the Bastendorffs for three weeks, from 24 September 1877, and nothing more was heard from her after mid-October. Scraps of clothing and a brooch found in the cellar were identified as Matilda's, although her brother Edward was unable to say if the body was definitely that of his sister.

The police interviewed Hannah Dobbs in prison. Indeed, it was she who first mentioned the name of 'Hacker'. Over the next few weeks, a series of discoveries unfolded that led to Hannah being charged with Matilda's murder in October of 1877. Her story made sad reading. The poorly educated daughter of a farm labourer, domestic service was one of the few jobs open to her. She later admitted, 'I never could resist the desire to dress well, and I never could bring myself to refuse money, food or clothes to those I thought needed them, even if I had to beg, borrow or steal to do so.'

Dismissed by her first employer for theft, stealing became part of her life.

Matilda Hacker was born in Canterbury and inherited property from her father. She lived with her sister Amelia and they were affectionately nicknamed the 'Canterbury Belles', from their habit of identically dressing in clothes better suited to younger women, rather than mature ladies. After Amelia died in 1873, Matilda took a house in Brighton. However, she left before her rental expired, so her landlord sued her for breaking the lease. To avoid this writ being served (and a subsequent summons for non-payment of rates in Kent), Matilda began a series of rapid flits from rented room to rented room in London: Woburn Place, Bedford Place, Chelsea, Mornington Crescent and finally Euston Square. To confuse the authorities further, she used various aliases: Stephens, Bell, Sycamore (various spellings) and Miss (H)Uish.

The trial of Hannah Dobbs began on 2 July. It exposed the casual arrangements at No. 4 Euston Square, where neither Severin nor his wife Mary appeared to take any interest in their tenants. Witness contradicted witness. Mary said Hannah had told her when Miss Hacker left – but Hannah said no, she'd been absent at the time. Hannah's intimate relationship with Peter, Severin's brother, was known before the trial, but it was further suggested, in court, that the prisoner was on intimate terms with her master too. This did little to improve her image in the eyes of the public or the jury. However, the judge declared that they must be sure of two things: that the body was that of Matilda; and, if so, that Miss Hacker had been murdered by Hannah. The jury took just half an hour to find her not guilty.

Hannah returned to prison to serve out the remainder of her sentence for theft. Following her release, on 8 August, she took up again with Peter. The following month adverts appeared for a pamphlet entitled *The Euston Square Mystery*, being

Hannah Dobbs. (Courtesy of Camden Local Studies and Archive Centre)

the 'extraordinary statement' of Hannah Dobbs. The publisher was Mr Purkess, owner of the *Illustrated Police News*. Among many startling revelations, Hannah accused the Bastendorffs of murder, blackmail, theft from tenants and barbaric cruelty. She insisted that Matilda had missed items from her room, and been killed by the Bastendorffs to prevent her contacting the police. Hannah implied that Miss Hacker had been shot; the rope found about her neck had been used to haul poor Matilda's body up into an attic, and to drag her back down into the cellar.

The story then becomes more lurid. Hannah told readers of *The Euston Square Mystery* that she'd discovered the body of Matilda Hacker, and that the Bastendorffs had told her that she'd be accused of being an accomplice if she went to the authorities. She also named another lodger – Mr Findlay – whom she said had vanished, the implication being he too had been murdered. Hannah went on to claim that she'd watched the family members beat a street urchin to death after he had taken refuge in their back-garden store, before the murderers fed his flesh to a lodger's dog. Joseph, a third brother, was accused of skinning another dog alive, its meat being thereafter cooked and eaten. Hannah also revealed that she and Severin had been in a sexual relationship for several months before she came to work at Euston Square, and that Severin had continued to visit her regularly at night, in her bedroom.

Severin denied everything in an affidavit and attempted to get an injunction to prevent publication, but Hannah had witnesses who could testify to the truth of her relationship with Bastendorff. That December he was tried for perjury on that single count. It emerged that Severin and Hannah had met and started their relationship in 1875, when Hannah was working in Torrington Square. When she thought she was pregnant with Severin's child, he'd told her (she said) to sleep with Peter so that he'd have to take responsibility. Severin was found guilty, and sentenced to twelve months' hard labour.

Following his release, Severin sued Purkess, still claiming that the pamphlet was libellous. A settlement was arrived at, with Bastendorff being awarded £500 and costs.

The Bastendorffs remained at No. 4 Euston Square after Severin's release from prison, but Severin was badly affected by his experiences. His business suffered and his marriage collapsed. He was twice committed to an asylum, escaping on the second occasion. His wife Mary took him to court in 1886, having suffered a violent beating during a dispute about money. Mary said her children (now abroad) were destitute, and applied to have Severin declared insane. The following May he was remanded, and charged 'with being a lunatic not under proper control', having made a statement to the police: 'I have been sent by Almighty God to claim £30,000. My brother Peter and his wife murdered Miss Hacker.' Severin died in Colney Hatch Asylum in 1909, having suffered from 'chronic mania over 21 years'.

What of Hannah Dobbs? After achieving further notoriety by allowing her waxwork to be exhibited at Madame Tussauds, she disappeared. Matilda Hacker's murder remains unsolved.

JANUARY 1880

A KILBURN MURDER

The First Time I Meet Her Will be the Last

ONE OF THE most violent murders in Kilburn's history happened on a busy street in full view of many passers-by.

John Wingfield was a thirty-four-year-old labourer, and his wife Mary was thirty-two. They'd been together for some years, but it was a difficult marriage and the couple finally separated in March 1879, when Mary moved into lodgings in Canterbury Road, taking one of their children with her. Since redeveloped, in 1880 Canterbury Road was a busy thoroughfare off Kilburn High Road, lined with houses, shops and a pub or two.

John was desperate for reconciliation. Jealous of Mary's friends, he began to stalk his wife. Mary shared her troubles with her landlady, Susan Goodrich – in particular, the fact that John had treated her badly. John often came past the house, but he never tried to see Mary until that January, when he knocked at the door on at least three occasions. The landlady sent him away with excuses. Ominously, he then told Susan that God had stopped him from striking his wife or he should have been under lock and key: 'the first time I meet her will be the last.'

When Mary left her lodgings around 10.30 a.m. on the morning of 27 January 1880, it's almost certain John was waiting for her. It was foggy, so perhaps she didn't spot him. He was seen running after Mary in nearby Denmark Road, with a knife in his hand, and as his wife stepped off the kerb John caught her, pulled her down, and knelt upon her shoulders with her head between his legs. At John's trial, passer-by Jesse Potter gave a graphic account of what happened next:

He was striking her all up the front part of her as hard as he could, all up the belly. I saw him strike three or four

Canterbury Road, Kilburn, looking towards Kilburn High Road.

Saxby and Farmer Works, where the murderer was captured. (Westinghouse)

blows. I did not then know that he had a knife in his hand, I saw it after. I then ran up to him and caught hold of him and pulled him off her by his collar. He made a strike at me and said 'I will serve you the same, you bastard, if you interfere with me.' I then stepped on the kerb away from him, and he stood on his legs and hit the knife right into her ear. Several people had come up by then. He pulled her head and shoulders right up off the ground by the knife and shook the head three times to get out the knife. Some other men came up. I appealed to them to help me, but they would not. They yelled 'police', 'stop' and 'murder'. The prisoner continued stabbing her about the head and face. He said, 'You know I love you, my girl; I don't like to see you in misery, I might as well finish you now,' and he put the knife on to her neck to cut her throat.

The press seemed surprised that no one did more to stop the attack. However, faced with a very angry – and seemingly crazy – man wielding a knife, what would most people do? Jesse was a remarkably brave man to try.

John inflicted at least fourteen mortal wounds over the space of three or four minutes, causing massive brain damage. Mary never regained consciousness, and died at St Mary's Hospital, Paddington. The doctor described ten wounds to her head and face, the most serious penetrating the right eyelid. John had used such force that the point of the knife had snapped off behind her right ear.

After he had cut Mary's throat, John stood up and spoke to Jesse, who was rooted to the spot. 'I prayed to God this should not happen last Sunday night, but it has now. I know I shall not have to live long, shall I? May the Lord have mercy on my poor soul.' The murderer then ran away, followed by the indomitable Jesse, heading towards the Kilburn High Road and into Saxby and Farmer's signalling works. John knew the layout well as he'd worked there for two years. He rushed into the carpenter's shop, still brandishing the knife and yelling, 'Show me the man that took my old woman to the Metropolitan Music Hall!' This seemed to be the root of the murderer's anger: as he stabbed his wife, John had repeatedly called on her, blaming her for going to the Metropolitan Music Hall and leaving his children at home.

Jesse quickly told the workmen what John had done. William Relf, the foreman, stepped forward and when John presented the weapon, handle forward, he took it. At the trial, Relf confirmed that John had worked as a timber washer at the company: 'I found him a steady, hardworking, respectable man.'

When he was arrested, John asked if his wife was dead. He continued:

> I went to the Metropolitan last night to see her; I went to bed at 2 o'clock this morning; I was up again at 4 o'clock; I waited to see her; I knelt down to pray to God last Sunday night, but this is done after all; God bless her, I love her still; now my poor children will have clean sheets to lie in and someone to look after them, poor little things.

At his trial, John sat with his head in his hands, in a 'very desponding and miserable state'. His defence lawyers said John was of 'unsound mind' when he attacked his wife, and that he had a previous history of mental instability. Evidence was given that John's sister had been confined to an asylum for three years. A doctor also testified to seeing John, about eighteen months previously, after an arrest for smashing the windows of his lodgings: 'He was in such a highly excited state that I had the impression that he really was a lunatic, from his violence and his manner generally.' When the judge began his summing up, John suddenly shrieked, 'Oh my head, oh my head!', and fell down in a fit. He was found guilty of murder nonetheless, sentenced to hang and removed from the court in 'an almost insensible condition'.

John Wingfield's execution was set for 22 March. A petition to the Home Office asking that his sentence be commuted on the grounds of probable insanity was rejected. In Newgate he was a model prisoner, and made a full confession of his guilt, saying he'd acted in a fit of jealous rage and was sorry for what he'd done. John's last words were 'God have mercy on me': he literally died with a prayer on his lips.

ONE A PENNY, TWO A PENNY, HOT CROSS BUNS!

On Good Friday, 30 March 1888, sixteen-year-old Cecilia Finch, the daughter of a Kilburn bus conductor, ate no fewer than twelve hot cross buns. Unfortunately, these swelled up in her stomach and obstructed her bowel. She died after one of her intestines collapsed. Poor Cecilia was buried a week later in Hampstead Cemetery.

THE GREAT GAS EXPLOSION AT TOTTENHAM COURT ROAD

SHORTLY AFTER 7 p.m. on 5 July 1880, a series of violent explosions off Tottenham Court Road sent pedestrians running for cover as the road surface erupted in flames and paving stones flew through the air. The force of the explosion – and the resulting damage – was similar to that of a bomb exploding, and it was a miracle that only two men, both gas company workmen, died. Many passers-by and residents were hurt, however, and hundreds of properties were damaged.

The gas company had recently completed the work of replacing an old main between Howland Street, running along Charlotte Street and across to Tottenham Court Road via Percy Street. There a junction was made with a second main, running eastward from the corner of Bayley Street. The first explosion was at this junction, outside the Bedford Head pub and hotel, where workmen were preparing to connect the mains. As the workmen tested the newly connected mains, the gas caught fire. Alfred Beavis, the man nearest the blast, became a human cannonball, blown 24ft down the 3ft-diameter gas main. He sustained dreadful injuries to

his left side, and multiple fractures to that arm and leg; his face was 'charred so as to be unrecognisable.' Fellow labourer William Burr was also very badly hurt but made it to a hospital, where doctors amputated his mangled right leg at the hip. Sadly, however, he died soon afterwards.

As the fire took hold, six more explosions followed: two in Percy Street, one at the junction of Percy Street and Charlotte Street, and three more moving north up Charlotte Street as far as Howland Street.

In Percy Street it was the houses on the south side that were mainly affected. Some of the properties were in mixed use as shops and private homes. The second explosion opened up a large chasm outside Nos 15, 16 and 17: 'Here the aspect of the houses can only be likened to that which would follow a bombardment.' The pavement sank as cellars beneath collapsed; bricks and timber were forced through basements, while goods were badly damaged by the stones that hurtled through the premises. Even more damage was done to Nos 5, 6 and 7, where basements were ripped open and foundations exposed.

Aftermath of the gas main explosion in Charlotte Street.

The force of this third explosion was so great that even roofs and chimneys were damaged, torn by paving stones thrown up into the air, some sailing over the houses to land on buildings behind. One stone, measuring 2ft by 6in, fell into an Italian carver's studio and smashed his models. More were found in the rooms of No. 5. Its occupants, and that of No. 6, emerged unscathed. Mr Elias Simmons, an antiques collector, described their lucky escape: 'My wife was sitting with her baby Bessie in her arms in the front drawing room,' he later said, 'next the street, and though terribly alarmed and shaken by the concussion, she was miraculously saved from being struck by the shower of granite paving-stones and concrete which was hurled through the windows and covered the floor all around her.'

Amazingly, she only had one small cut, though all the windows and the roof skylight were shattered. The floors were covered with broken glass and china mixed with plaster torn from great holes in the walls. As a result of this damage, Simmons auctioned part of his collection: furniture, china, ivories, statues and bronzes were soon on sale.

An eyewitness wrote of his terrifying experience in Percy Street:

I felt myself lifted from the ground, and the next moment I was lying among the debris at the bottom of a deep hole in the roadway. The gas nearly choked me, and with much difficulty I scrambled out of the trench. A horse and cart were blown into the cavity, the poor animal being shockingly injured, whilst the cart was smashed to pieces by the falling stones and bricks. A thick red dust enveloped the street. Some children were also thrown into the trench, and some of these I helped extricate and carry to their homes.

Many of the injured never sought medical attention. Around twenty-five were sent to the nearby Middlesex Hospital, and after a couple of days all but six had been discharged. Reports of the number of houses damaged varied from 200 to 400 – and around thirteen were ruled structurally unsafe.

Workmen in Charlotte Street also had a narrow escape when a length of loose coping crashed into the basement area. The sum of £81 was raised for the 'sufferers', but the fund was closed after 'liberal arrangements' were made for the injured. The gas company, while accepting no liability, agreed to repair property and meet claims for personal injury.

The cause of this dreadful calamity was revealed at the subsequent inquest. There the foreman, William Hawkes, freely admitted applying a lighted match, given him by poor William Burr, to a test pipe at the site of the first explosion. He'd checked first, he said, and believed that there was no gas in the main – adding the incredible statement that he 'didn't know' that a mixture of gas and air was dangerous. The verdict was therefore one of accidental death: that Hawkes' 'ignorant' application of the flame had caused the explosion.

But the new main was meant to be empty – so how had the mixture accumulated in the pipe? The inquest ruled that it had entered via a faulty valve at the Howland Street junction. However, this last fact could not be verified, as the valve had been destroyed by the last explosion. Other official reports agreed with the inquest's findings. Trade journal *The Engineer* concluded: 'Rarely has so much damage been done over so considerable an area in the centre of a large town with so little loss of life.'

AD 1884

A BIZARRE MENAGERIE

ELEPHANTS IN A FIX

It's not often the streets of London echo to the trumpeting of elephants, but that's what happened in Kentish Town in March 1884. Sanger's Circus was booked to set up its tents near Gospel Oak. At around 1.45 p.m. on the 8th, a train carrying artistes, horses and four elephants arrived at the Kentish Town Midland station. The elephants were unloaded in the sidings (on the site of Regis Road today), where they had to exit via the end of their truck. The first pair, Jim and Rose, calmly made their way into the yard for a long drink. But the second pair, Palm and Ida, were frightened by a sudden noise. They panicked, pushing over their keeper Charles Miles (and breaking his collarbone) before stampeding towards the locked station gates, which broke 'like match-wood'. Turning up Highgate Road, the elephants knocked over another man, who fortunately 'was more frightened than hurt, as he was seen to get up and run away, leaving his hat behind him'. It was amazing that the beasts didn't collide with any of the carts, buses or tramcars on the busy main road. Palm

and Ida got as far as the Vine pub, where a group of people fell over one another in their frantic attempts to escape (resulting in a second broken collarbone). The tuskers bolted along the narrow College Lane, which ran parallel to and behind the houses of Kentish Town Road. They got as far as the Baptist Chapel on the corner with Chetwynd Road, but failed to get over the chapel wall before making a minor detour into Twisden Road. Here they knocked over, but didn't seriously hurt, a child.

By now they'd travelled around a mile, and were being chased by hundreds of people. The frightened elephants rushed up Chetwynd Road and Cathcart Hill to Junction Road, then across into Francis Terrace. This was a cul-de-sac that ended in a boarded-up passage to Pemberton Terrace, between Nos 29 and 31. They broke through into the Terrace, where the chase ended: the passage floor between the two houses gave way and first one and then the other elephant tumbled into the cellar below. And there they stayed for nearly two hours. The police soon arrived with workmen, who set about enlarging the opening and constructing a slope that

1. They Break Loose and Run Gaily Down Cathcart Hill.—2. They Enter a Passage Leading from Francis Terrace to Pemberton Gardens.—3. They Fall Into a Cellar in Pemberton Gardens.—4. Here They Remain.—5. Until the Arrival of Help.—6. When They are Pulled Out of the Cellar, and Go Off Contentedly with their Rescuers.

THE STRANGE ADVENTURES OF TWO RUNAWAY ELEPHANTS IN KENTISH TOWN, LONDON

the elephants could walk up. Although one paper reported that 'the capture was not completed without the aid of a bun', the keepers actually fed Palm and Ida loaves of bread to encourage them up the incline, while Jim and Rose helped pull their companions to freedom. Then all four elephants were chained together and walked to Gospel Oak, 'not any the worse for their extraordinary adventure' and accompanied by a huge crowd. Sanger was a keen publicist, but even he couldn't have thought up a better stunt to advertise his show! The circus played to record numbers all week.

HAPPY OF HAMPSTEAD

In August 1926, an equally bizarre sight greeted residents at the Vale of Health Hotel on Hampstead Heath. The hotel's owner Fred Gray claimed a mysterious 'monster' with 'the head of a gorilla and a bark like that of a dog' had been living in the nearby pond!

On the evening of the 25th, an angler rushed into the hotel claiming to have caught the creature on his line. His catch was carried into the hotel and put in an iron tank, to be identified the following day as a young seal. Fred Gray, who also owned the fairground by the side of the hotel, told the press this wasn't the first time a seal had been found in the pond, and speculated that (like the others) this seal had reached Hampstead from the sea, by swimming up the River Fleet (which was connected with the Thames). He continued: 'There is no doubt that there are other big creatures in the pond. We can hear them, and on a fine day, from the hotel veranda, we can see them, through a glass, sunning themselves.'

After initially refusing food, the seal started to eat huge quantities of whiting. Doubling in weight, it was christened 'Happy of Hampstead' and enjoyed basking in the sunshine. About a week later, another report appeared in the press. A second 'creature' had been caught: 'it fought like a lion' but died almost immediately it was landed. Gray described it as about 5ft long and brown: it was probably a seal, but 'with a lot of scales'. Unfortunately for science, however, Gray said that the body had since disappeared, removed by the man who caught it.

But it was all a scam. It's almost certain the second incident never happened: it was dreamed up by Gray to keep people interested and further boost trade. Even his description was guaranteed to tantalise, with its 'scaly monster' overtones. The first seal was real enough, but was probably never in the pond as it would have been impossible to land it with a conventional rod and tackle. There was also no way it could have swum up to Hampstead, traversing the sewer that now contained the Fleet River. And how fortunate that there happened to be a prepared tank at the hotel, waiting to accommodate Happy! Charlie Abbott, Gray's grandson, admitted many years later that the seal had been brought from the Wash in Norfolk to Hampstead in a fairground lorry. What happened to 'Happy' is not recorded, but Charlie believed that the seal was eventually returned to the sea in the same way it had appeared.

MISCHIEVOUS MONKEYS IN HAMPSTEAD

For a while, the publican at the Bull and Bush pub, just a short distance from the Vale of Health, kept monkeys in a cage in his garden. On the afternoon of Friday, 19 August 1898, two escaped. They stayed, hidden, on Hampstead Heath until noon the following Sunday, when they were spotted by some boys who threw stones at them. The monkeys 'jabbered and made faces at their assailants', swinging from tree to tree and easily eluding anyone who climbed after them, tempted by a cash reward for their capture. On Monday, however, the monkeys gave themselves up, returning to the Bull and Bush, 'forlorn, dirty-looking, and evidently very miserable.'

However, within days they'd escaped again – taking two more monkeys with them! The four explored Hampstead Heath, in the area between the Bull and Bush and the Spaniards Inn, venturing into 'the well-kept grounds and conservatories' of nearby houses, doing considerable damage and scaring the occupants in the process. The publican, reluctantly, at last gave permission for the animals to be shot. Three were killed outright; the fourth, called Joey, was slightly wounded, and made his way back to his cage. It was reported that he didn't seem 'much the worse for his hair-breadth escape'.

AD 1886

THE BRECKNOCK ROAD SHOOTING

IT WAS AROUND 4.30 p.m. on 10 June 1886. Frances Hardy gasped as she spotted John William Bowes lying on her shop floor, bleeding from a wound to his head. Then she became aware that there was a man crouching behind the shop counter. As he stood up, she realised he had a gun.

About eighteen months ago, her brother Robert had taken over a chemist and druggist's business at No. 165 Brecknock Road, on the corner with Lady Margaret Road. The shop also doubled as a post office, where Frances worked, with a qualified chemist, John Bowes, employed as Hardy's assistant. Frances had been in the room behind the shop, brewing the usual afternoon tea she shared with John, when she heard a gunshot. Rushing back, she came face-to-face with the gunman – who then fired for a second time, the bullet grazing her face and forehead. Frances turned and ran, out through a side door and into the street. There were plenty of people about. Alfred Partell heard two loud reports, and then Frances's cries of 'Murder!' He chased a man who ran out of the chemist's, but couldn't catch him. Returning to Brecknock Road, Alfred confirmed that Bowes had been shot.

Chief Inspector James Millward happened to be around the corner and had watched a man run along Ospringe Road and into No. 15. So, when he was approached by Partell, the two men went and knocked on the door.

It was the home of the Finch family, where the widowed owner Charlotte took in lodgers. Her three children lived with her: twenty-three-year-old Sarah Valentine, nineteen-year-old George Vincent Heneage and Charles, age three. Millward and Partell were told that George had recently come home, but they couldn't find him when they searched the house. The policeman returned to the shop, where he found that Bowes had been carried into the back room. He died shortly afterwards, the cause of death a bullet wound to his left temple. George Vincent Heneage Finch was now wanted for murder. A second search of No. 15 began. This time Millward was accompanied by Sergeant Moon (who had helped rescue the elephants trapped in Pemberton Gardens). Almost by accident, the two men looked up at the ceiling above the toilet. There they noticed a trap

The Penny Illustrated Paper *covers the Brecknock Road murder.*

door which had been displaced. Moon, who was the smaller man, stood on the toilet seat and pushed the trap door open. Inside he found George Finch crouching in the small space by the cistern. He was still holding the gun.

Millward spoke to the young man.

'Give me that revolver, Finch.'

George replied, 'It was entirely an accident.'

'I don't know whether it was an accident or not, but if it was it would be better for you to give up the revolver at once.'

'If I do, you will take me!' said George.

A second policeman tried talking George into surrendering, but had no success.

At last, the sergeant said, 'Will you give me the revolver?'

'Good God!' the man replied. 'I don't know what to do. I won't give it up. It was an accident!'

The wanted man finally surrendered when the police began sawing through the floorboards of the room above. Mrs Finch's servant said he'd spotted George holding a revolver in his room a few weeks before the murder. George replied that he'd had it about a year, and that 'Ma' knew all about it.

But when George's mother spoke to the press she denied this claim. Instead, she told of mental illness in the family: an uncle who died in an asylum and a cousin who 'studied too much, and went insane'. She voiced no compassion for the Bowes family. Her concern was only for her son. George, she said, had wanted for nothing. He had a good education and the right to a coat of arms (there was a distant link to Lord Aylesford's family) – all now wasted opportunities. 'It is too shocking!' she told reporters:

> I don't know what has come over my son lately. He has certainly not been right in his mind. He has threatened to take his life many times lately. It is a very sad affair altogether, and I am sure I do not know what made him commit such a rash act.

By all accounts George was a talented artist, but about a year ago he had abandoned his studies and decided to become a theatrical agent and acting coach. He started 'The Royalty Dramatic Company', but it struggled. Their first production was put on that April in Camden Town, at the Royal Park Hall. George ran up debts as the show went on, debts which his mother helped to pay.

Since then he'd generally failed to show up for performances or rehearsals. When a reporter interviewed neighbours, they mentioned George's 'idle habits' and outbursts of temper, but to most he appeared 'genial in an unassuming way and steady, generally esteemed.'

Given the overwhelming evidence, it was inevitable that George Vincent Heneage Finch should be charged with the murder of Bowes, as well as with the attempted murder of Frances Hardy and with robbery (he'd reached over the counter and taken a cash box containing around £7 in coins). Both box and money were found in Finch's hiding place. However, he never stood trial: a postponement was agreed in order to gather medical evidence of his mental state, and there it was revealed that only a week before the shooting Finch had been seen in the garden, on his hands and knees, eating grass. He was subsequently ruled insane and ordered to be detained at Her Majesty's pleasure.

Why did Finch kill Bowes? The case wasn't as straightforward as early reports made out. These said that Finch fired the shot during a robbery when John tried to stop him stealing the cash box. But a local errand boy and a postman both said they'd seen Finch and Bowes talking for some fifteen minutes before Finch fired the fatal shot. Though neither could hear the conversation, it was clear from their body language that the men weren't arguing. Finch later said that a 'very nice young fellow' in a post office nearby had offered him financial help, but in the end he couldn't get the money. Was the man Bowes? Did George snatch the money because he thought Bowes 'owed' it to him?

George was sent to Broadmoor, the asylum for the insane. The 1911 census still shows him as an inmate at the age of forty-four, but he was subsequently released and worked as a carpenter.

'POOR LITTLE TIGGIE'

The Murder of Phoebe and Tiggie Hogg

THE POLICEMAN AND a young clerk recoiled in horror at the dreadful sight revealed by the flickering match. Phoebe Hogg lay sprawled across a pile of rubble, her head almost severed from her body. This gruesome discovery was made in Crossfield Road, Hampstead, at around 7 p.m. on 24 October 1890. About 1.5 miles away, Elizabeth Andrews left her employer's home in Hamilton Terrace, St John's Wood, at 7.30 p.m. and noticed a perambulator abandoned outside the house. It would later transpire that this had been the vehicle used to transport Phoebe's corpse.

The body of her daughter, eighteen-month-old Phoebe Hanslope Hogg (affectionately known as Tiggie), was discovered the following morning, lying face down in a bed of nettles in a field at the corner of Cannon Hill and Finchley Road.

The subsequent trial revealed a tragic love triangle involving Frank Hogg, his wife Phoebe and his mistress, Mary Pearcey. Mr John Pearcey lived with Mary in Camden Town (where Mary was known as Mrs Pearcey, although they never married); Frank Hogg's

family owned a grocer's shop in the neighbourhood, at No. 87 King (now Plender) Street, where Frank first met Mary as a customer. They began to have an affair – and Mary's husband left when he became aware of it.

It seems that Frank met Mary and his future wife, Phoebe Styles, at around the same time. Phoebe was born in Chorley Wood, north of London, in 1860. By 1881 she was working as a nurse for a family in Arkwright Road, Hampstead. It's not known how she met Frank, but they were engaged for a couple of years before marrying in November 1888. Their only child, Phoebe Hanslope Hogg, was born the following July. It would appear Frank 'did the right thing' by marrying his pregnant fiancé – but he wasn't happy about it, and kept on seeing Mary as his mistress. She wrote to Frank just before his wedding: 'I would rather see you married fifty times over – yes, I could bear that far better than parting with you for ever.'

The Hogg family home was at rented rooms at No. 141 Prince of Wales Road, where Frank, Phoebe and their baby daughter lived on the second floor. Frank's widowed mother and sister,

The Hampstead murder in all its awful detail.
(IPN, 1 November 1890)

Clara, occupied the floor below. Frank continued seeing Mary Pearcey – in fact, he even had her latchkey so he could come and go as he pleased; 'I visited Mrs Pearcey about two or three times a week,' he later confessed, 'and must admit I was on intimate terms with her, but I do not think my wife knew anything about it.' He even introduced Mary to Phoebe, and the Hogg family spent Christmas 1889 at Mary's home. But Phoebe had begun to suspect that her husband was having an affair. In February 1890 she briefly left Frank, and went to stay with relatives. She told her sister Martha, 'I have never been happy since I entered that house.'

At around 3 p.m. on 24 April, events approached their tragic climax. Phoebe went to see Mary Pearcey at her home, No. 2 Priory Street, off Camden Road. She was wheeling baby Tiggie in a 'bassinette perambulator', a large wicker-work basket body on a metal chassis. It is probable that Phoebe had decided to confront Mary about her relationship with Frank. She arrived at Priory Street half an hour later and left the pram in the hall. Mary Pearcey lived on the ground floor, renting rooms overlooking a communal yard. At around 4 p.m. neighbours reported hearing a 'commotion' in the kitchen: the sound of breaking glass, and of a baby crying. Then all was quiet.

Inside, Mary had taken the poker and shattered Phoebe's skull. She then set about cutting off her head, which was left attached to the body by only a thin section of skin and muscle. Baby Tiggie was probably suffocated, although it is possible that she died from exposure in the field where she was found.

Shortly after 6 p.m. a neighbour saw Mary wheeling a heavily loaded pram along Priory Street. She was spotted again at around 6.30 p.m., turning along Prince of Wales Road. She was heading towards Haverstock Hill – which meant that she actually wheeled her awful burden past the dead woman's home. The police later reconstructed what they believed happened next: that Mary went up Adelaide Road, before turning down unlighted streets towards Eton Avenue. The neighbourhood was still being developed at the time, and there were open fields close to Swiss Cottage. The roadway and pavement of Crossfield Road were unfinished, in a muddy and broken-up state. The police decided that Mary probably hadn't intended to dump Phoebe's body here: it is more likely that the pram tipped up and the body fell out. Then, after continuing to St John's Wood and abandoning the bassinette, Mary had returned home, gathered up Tiggie's body and set off to dispose of the second corpse. However, although the police concluded otherwise, it is possible that the baby was in the pram, underneath or on top of Phoebe's body, the whole time. If so, she must have been well wrapped, as Tiggie's clothes weren't bloodstained. Mary could have carried the toddler's body on from Hamilton Terrace, until it became too heavy for her to continue. Unfortunately, a railway worker who said he'd seen a woman carrying a suspicious-looking bundle along Finchley Road was unable to identify Mary at a later date.

Mary, of course, wasn't at Priory Street when Frank Hogg called at around 10.20 p.m. He'd spent the day shifting furniture (giving him a perfect alibi, as he'd been working with a companion). When he got home he wasn't unduly worried to find Phoebe absent: her father was seriously ill and the couple had agreed that Phoebe would go to Chorley Wood if needed. He left for his in-laws early the next morning, before the news of a body's discovery had become common knowledge. Clara Hogg, however, was convinced that the body was her sister-in-law – and persuaded Mrs Pearcey to accompany her to Hampstead police station. There Clara identified Phoebe's body, despite Mary's frantic attempts to pull her away.

Seeing this, the police began to grow suspicious. They asked Mary if they could search her house at No. 2 Priory Road. There they found a bloodstained poker and several knives. A pool of blood on the carpet marked the spot where Phoebe's throat had been cut as she lay on the floor, unconscious. There was more blood on the walls and ceiling of the kitchen, and 'great clots' on the curtains. Two window panes were broken. Mary was arrested, but seemed unconcerned; 'she whistled to herself and assumed an air of complete indifference.' At this date there was

Mary Pearcey in the dock. (Daily Graphic, *28 October 1890*)

no DNA evidence, or even detailed information about blood or fingerprint evidence. The medical experts couldn't positively identify which knife had been used to cut poor Phoebe's throat, and Mary variously ascribed the bloodstains to a nose bleed and to her efforts to kill an infestation of mice. The closest Mary got to an admission was to tell a woman searching her at the police station that, 'Mrs Hogg made a remark which I did not like. One word brought up another – but there, perhaps I had better not say any more.'

THE SENTENCE

The judge summed up the case at the trial. While no one saw Mary Pearcey kill Phoebe Hogg, he said, that didn't mean she was innocent. Mary's letters to Frank had been examined, and the judge concluded that they 'showed her passionate and ungovernable: he would not call it love, but lust.' He concluded: 'You [Mrs Pearcey] have been the instrument in taking away the life of a woman whose only offence towards you was that she was married to a man on whom you had set your unholy passion.' Mary replied, 'I am innocent of the charge.' The former view held sway, and she was sentenced to be hanged.

After Frank Hogg's affair with Mary Pearcey was revealed, he became the object of public hatred: 'no man ever gave himself a viler or more loathsome character,' said one source. The funeral of Phoebe and her daughter took place at Finchley Cemetery on Sunday 2 November, 'in the midst of scenes which cannot be considered otherwise than most disgraceful'. A large police presence assembled outside Clatworthy's, the undertakers, at No. 92 Camden High Street, but they were vastly outnumbered by a crowd of 3,000 to 4,000 spectators. When Frank, accompanied by his brother Edwin and Edwin's wife, drove up in a cab the crowd pushed forward, shouting rude remarks and insults. The police advised that the funeral procession get underway as soon as possible. The only other mourners were Phoebe's sister Martha and niece Elizabeth Styles. Another disorderly crowd had assembled at the cemetery gates and 'an unseemly rush' was made to enter the chapel. A single polished elm coffin enclosed both Phoebe and Tiggie: 'a remarkably fine child, ruddy even in death, lies on the mother's bosom.' The clergyman made no reference to how they had died, but once the service was over the crowd again turned on Frank Hogg and the police were hard-pressed to prevent him being assaulted. Mother and daughter were buried in the unconsecrated part of the cemetery.

Unsuccessful petitions were raised for Mary's sentence to be commuted. Mary declared that Frank had nothing to do with the murders and she maintained her innocence to her mother: 'do not fret for me, as I have not got anything to be afraid of,' she said. Mary was hanged at Newgate Prison at 8 a.m. on 23 December 1890. A few minutes before the noose was placed round her neck, the chaplain asked, 'Do you admit the justice of your sentence?'

'Yes; but the greater part of the evidence was false.'

'Then you mean to say you are guilty?'

But Mary did not reply. The crowd outside the prison cheered when they learned the sentence had been carried out. She was buried inside the prison grounds in the recycled grave of a murderer executed in 1867. Her coffin was loaded with lime and water was poured through holes in the lid to accelerate the destruction of the corpse. It's not known what happened to Frank Hogg, but given the level of public animosity towards him he almost certainly left the neighbourhood.

AD 1893

ANOTHER FATEFUL LOVE TRIANGLE

The Regent Square Murder

ISABELLA MONTAGUE (or Bessie, to her friends) was a popular twenty-five-year-old singer and dancer in the chorus at the Empire Theatre of Varieties, Leicester Square. In the show *Round the Town* she rode across the stage on a bicycle 'made for two', using the stage name 'Daisy'. Bessie was nineteen when she met and became engaged to Leo Percy, an instrument maker and inventor. But his parents disapproved, and although the couple stayed together they weren't able to marry.

In 1893 Bessie called off the engagement and became friendly with Samuel Garcia, a twenty-seven-year-old stockbroker. Bessie was then living at No. 18 Regent Square, near King's Cross, with her brother John and another member of the chorus troupe, Mrs Augusta Herbert, the widow of a clerk. Each evening Samuel met Bessie and Augusta at the stage door and escorted them home. On Wednesday, 20 September 1893, they arrived at No. 18 just before 1 a.m. and Augusta went upstairs to light the fire. Bessie and Samuel decided to go for a walk around the square – unaware that Leo was following them. Suddenly, in a

jealous rage, her former fiancé pulled a revolver out of his pocket and fired two shots at Samuel. One shot passed harmlessly through Samuel's silk hat, but the second hit him in the head. Bessie screamed and tried to run away, but a third bullet hit her in the back. Leo then turned the gun on himself. The murder was witnessed by a neighbour

Bessie Montague. (Penny Illustrated, 30 September 1893)

at No. 24: she had been sitting on the balcony waiting for her husband, who also worked late. She watched the happy young couple walking in the square, and saw them being followed by Garcia; as she watched, he fired at close range before shooting himself in the mouth. PC Lorie was on patrol nearby and also heard the shots. He found the two men's bodies, their blood and brains staining the pavement outside No. 28 Regent Square. Percy still held a heavy calibre 'black bulldog' revolver in his hand. But PC Lorie thought that Bessie had merely fainted, as he couldn't see any wound. He summoned two cabs and the

2. The late Leo Percy.
3. Samuel Garcia.
4. Miss Herbert, "Daisy's" friend.
5. Mrs. Winterbotham, who saw Percy shoot "Daisy," Garcia, and himself.
6. Corner of Regent Square, where the murders and suicide were committed.

Details from the Regent Square murder. (Penny Illustrated, 30 September 1893)

three victims were taken to the Royal Free Hospital in Gray's Inn Road. Bessie and Samuel were pronounced dead on arrival: she from internal bleeding, he from brain damage. Leo died about forty-five minutes later. On Thursday morning, vast crowds of people came to see the scene of the tragedy. At the inquest on Saturday, after hearing the evidence, the jury gave a verdict of wilful murder, and of suicide while temporarily insane.

This had all the hallmarks of a common Victorian story: the immorality and infidelity of a young actress, and the vengeance of her rival. But Bessie Montague was a hard-working, well-mannered young woman who lived quietly and regularly attended St Peter's, the local church in the square (since demolished). She had an honourable engagement with Leo Percy, and they would have married had his parents not believed that they were too young. After their relationship broke up, Percy became obsessed with the young singer. A few weeks before the murder, learning that Bessie had kissed another man, and suffering from depression, Leo had taken a large dose of laudanum. It didn't kill him, but Leo told a friend he wished it had. His brother said that Leo had recently appeared very weak and nervous, and that he spent long periods of time just staring into space. Just before the incident he had written to his family:

Dear Father,

I have no doubt that by the time you receive this you will know all, should what I expect occur. I can bear it no longer – the pain and humiliation is too great, so it is best ended. I determined long ago that none but I should have her, and I should have been dead long ago but for your sake. Forgive me any pain I may cause you. I hope you will forgive me,

- Your affectionate son,

Leo.

Leo Percy had been living in lodgings at No. 29 Swinton Street, near Regent Square. His landlady, Mary Richards, said that he was a remarkably quiet, unassuming and well-behaved young man. He had told her that he loved a woman far better than life itself, and that he would be prepared to die over and over again for her. His father, Stephen Percy, had been born in Hungary and was the manager of the Stentor Telephone Mouthpiece Company. When reporters called at the family home, No. 23 Regent Square – only a few doors away from Bessie's home – the family were in shock and refused to say anything.

Samuel Barnett Garcia had been born in Glasgow. He was the only son of Philip Henry Garcia, a well-known florist in Covent Garden. In 1893 he was living with his uncle at No. 1 Vernon Chambers, Southampton Row, in Bloomsbury. It was thought that he had recently made a lot of money on the stock market, but after his death and probate he only left £83. He was buried on Sunday 24 September at the Portuguese Burial Ground in Mile End Road. The following Tuesday, Bessie's funeral attracted a crowd of thousands. Her family and friends from the theatre attended the service at St Peter's church in Regent Square. Then the hearse, followed by a mourning coach, went to Finchley Cemetery. Leo Percy had been buried there quietly the previous day.

THE BAKER IN THE OVEN

AT AROUND 11 p.m. on 10 November 1898, Conrad Berndt went downstairs to start his shift in the bake-house at No. 82 William Street, off Hampstead Road. (This neighbourhood has since been redeveloped.) He was usually on his own, but tonight there was a second man present: Johann Schneider. Schneider ignored Conrad, who shrugged and turned to cut the dough; after all, it was none of his business if his employer, William Ross, had allowed Johann to stay the night. Berndt lodged with the Ross family above the baker's shop and was keeping company with Ross's eighteen-year-old niece Eva. Like Ross, Berndt was born in Germany. He was about twenty years old, a tall, quiet young man who everyone liked.

William Ross had moved his bakery business from Kentish Town in the mid-1890s. He was doing well and could number among his customers many of the wealthy residents of nearby Regent's Park, including Sir Blundell Maple MP and George Sims, the novelist. A competitor had recently made him an offer of £700 for the goodwill of his business alone. He could afford to be generous to Schneider, an old employee who'd fallen on hard times. Ross was woken as usual for his shift at around 3.15 a.m., but when he went downstairs it wasn't Berndt who greeted him but Schneider.

'Where's Conrad?' he asked.

'He's gone to bed: he feels ill,' said Johann.

'It's fortunate you're here: you can do his work,' replied William.

The two men went to the bake-house, where Ross bent down in front of the furnace to adjust the flour scales. He later remembered being struck a violent blow on the head from behind. Standing up, he turned and saw Schneider with

Johann Schneider. (Penny Illustrated, *24 December 1898)*

a knife in his hand. Ross's head was reeling, but he managed to run up the stairs nonetheless. Schneider grabbed him as he ran, and there was a violent struggle during which Ross's hands were badly cut as he tried to grasp the knife. Reaching the front door, he flung it open, shouting 'Murder!' Schneider then fled, escaping through an opening used for flour deliveries, and running off towards Euston Road.

The police found Ross leaning against the shop door, bleeding heavily from his wounds. They thought they were dealing with a violent assault – but the truth was much worse. An attempt had been made to clean the bake-house, but there was 'blood on the walls, on the dough for the new bread and on the made loaves. Still more ominous was the horrible burning smell that emanated from the baker's oven. When the iron door was opened a doubled-up human body was seen, already partially cremated.'

Poor Conrad Berndt! He had been hired by Ross when Schneider left. Schneider found it hard to get more work, and decided that Berndt was the cause of his problems. He'd attacked Conrad with a knife, a hatchet and a life preserver (a small cosh). There were signs in the room of a dreadful life-and-death struggle. The police threw water into the oven to cool it, and the body was gently pulled towards the door. The features were by now unrecognisable: Berndt was identified by items of charred clothing and his distinctive belt buckles. He died from a fractured skull and was unconscious – but horribly, he wasn't dead when Johann put him in the oven.

Ross told a reporter that 'he thanked Providence that he had escaped with

The bake-house and oven where Berndt was cremated. (Lloyds Weekly Newspaper, *13 November 1898*)

his life.' He believed Schneider's motive, so far as he was concerned, had been robbery: while the household slept, Johann had been upstairs and ransacked several rooms. He'd attacked Ross only because he thought Ross was going to check the furnace.

Schneider was arrested almost immediately, but before the police became aware that a crime had been committed. Around 3.30 a.m. two constables saw him near Tolmer Square: 'he was panting and wild-looking about the face; he looked frightened, as if he was afraid of meeting someone.' They gave chase when Johann turned and ran, noting that he threw something away before he was finally caught near Euston Square station. The trio retraced their steps and found a bloodstained knife. When he was charged, Scheinder said, 'I know nothing about it; I do not know the shop.'

It emerged that Schneider (who was also from Germany) had several aliases: Richard or Johann Mandelkow; Mandeckow; Montague; and Ricketts. At the police court he created a sensation when he fell down in the dock, his collapse later diagnosed as a hysterical rather than an epileptic fit. He was so distressed that the case was adjourned. A slightly built man, with a pale, thin face, short bushy beard and moustache, one report claimed that he didn't look 'capable of committing such an atrocious crime except in a state of frenzy.' He was committed for trial, but seemed to take little interest in the proceedings. A neighbour, the man who had given Schneider the knife, said Johann was 'morose, downcast, and absent-minded, depressed because of his poverty and because he could not find work, and he has three children and a wife.' But the burden of medical opinion was that Schneider was not insane and he was sentenced to be hanged. The verdict was translated into German, to make sure he understood. Schneider passed a restless night before his execution. He refused his breakfast and then, 'overcome with grief and fear, had to be assisted from the cell to the scaffold'. His last words were, 'Jesus Christ, forgive me all my wickedness and sins.'

REPERCUSSIONS

Crowds flocked to the scene of the crime – not to buy bread, but to peer through the grating (Schneider's escape route), trying to catch a glimpse of the oven. Trade fell away to almost nothing. Facing ruin, a subscription fund was started by the Master Bakers' Protection Society, and by late January it stood at just under £600. Ross had already decided on a fresh start and opened a new bakery near Holloway – no doubt helped by a further £200 given to him by a second trade organisation. When Conrad Berndt was buried, thousands of people watched the cortège pass by. The Master Bakers' paid for the grave and a memorial, but deducted these costs from the final amount passed over to Ross. By contrast, nothing was done for poor Schneider's widow. It was reported that she entered service and was forced to place her three children in a Roman Catholic orphanage. Her husband's waxwork appeared in Tussaud's Chamber of Horrors just a few days after his trial and conviction. One paper also said that Ross had sold them the bread oven.

THE GIRL IN THE SAILOR'S HAT

The Camden Town Murder

EMILY ELIZABETH DIMMOCK was born in 1884 in the village of Standon, near Bishops Stortford in Hertfordshire. After working as a chambermaid, and in a straw-hat factory in Luton, she ran away to London at the end of 1904. There she adopted the name 'Phyllis Dimmock', and began work as a prostitute. By 1906 she was living with Henry Biddle, a sailor from Portsmouth. One photograph shows her in his Prince of Wales uniform, but their relationship didn't last long. The following year Phyllis moved in with Bert Shaw in Camden Town, living at No. 50 Great (now Royal) College Street. Next she moved to No. 29 St Paul's Road (now Agar Grove). Bert was a cook on the Midland Railway, preparing food in the buffet car on the train from London to Sheffield. As he left for work in the afternoon, returning the following day, Phyllis was free to socialise in local pubs such as The Rising Sun on the Euston Road and The Eagle at the corner of Great College Street, opposite the present Camden Town Overground station. While he was away she slipped into her old ways and took men back to the flat to earn some extra cash.

On the morning of 12 September 1907, Bert came home to find his mother, who had come to visit, talking to the landlady. Apparently Phyllis wouldn't answer the door to their flat. A dreadful sight awaited Bert when he forced the connecting door to their bedroom. Phyllis lay naked on the bed, her throat cut from ear to ear. There was blood everywhere. Detective Inspector Neil from Scotland Yard was put in charge of the case. In the absence of any defensive wounds or signs of a struggle, he concluded Phyllis had been killed, with a single blow from a sharp knife, while she was sleeping. From the signs of rigor mortis and analysis of stomach contents, it was estimated that Phyllis had died between 3 a.m. and 5 a.m. the previous morning.

The police found an important clue: a postcard addressed to Phyllis. The sender suggested meeting on 9 September in The Rising Sun, but rather than giving the pub's name the author drew a picture of a rising sun. The newspapers reproduced the distinctive card and asked if anyone recognised the handwriting. A young woman called Ruby Young came forward and said it

Camden Town murder house and Emily Dimmock.

looked like the work of Robert Wood, who she'd been involved with for about three years. Wood was a thirty-year-old stained-glass artist at the Sand and Blast Manufacturing Company in Gray's Inn Road. Born in Scotland, the son of a print compositor on *The Scotsman* newspaper, the Woods moved to London where his father got work with the publisher Eyre and Spottiswode. In 1907 Robert was living with his family at No. 12 Frederick Street, near King's Cross.

Wood was arrested on 4 October. He admitted he'd written the postcard but said he'd only met Phyllis for the first time on the Friday before the murder. 'The Camden Town Murder' made all the headlines and large crowds attended the Old Bailey trial on 10 December 1907. Robert Wood had been leading a double life: he was a well-respected artist by day and someone who kept company with prostitutes by night. Witnesses gave evidence that

Wood had in fact known Phyllis for at least fifteen months. A work colleague of Wood's and his partner, Ruby Young, both told the jury that Robert had asked them to provide an alibi by lying about where he'd been on the evening of the murder. But several people had seen Wood and Phyllis together in The Eagle. Wood's father, brother and a neighbour all said that he'd returned home just before midnight.

Wood sat quietly drawing while the evidence was heard. He was defended by the charismatic barrister Edward Marshall Hall. A change in the law in 1898 meant the accused could give evidence. But no one had elected to do so – presumably fearing that they might incriminate themselves and also opening them up to cross-examination. Marshall Hall put Wood on the stand, a decision that could have proved fatal. Wood was a poor witness, speaking as if he was performing in amateur dramatics rather than fighting for his life. He admitted he was with Phyllis on the evening of 11 September but said he'd left her about 11 p.m. in The Eagle and gone home. Asked why he hadn't come forward after the murder, Wood replied that he hadn't wanted his sick father to know he was visiting prostitutes. The judge's summing up suggested he believed Wood was guilty, but then he concluded: 'In my judgement, strong as the suspicion is in this case, I do not think that the prosecution has brought the case home near enough to the accused.' He was interrupted by loud cheers from the public gallery. The jury returned a verdict after only fifteen minutes, finding Robert Wood not guilty.

But if Wood didn't kill Emily Dimmock, then who did? Inspector Neil always believed Wood was the murderer, but the case will probably never be solved. In 1907, the method of calculating the time of death was not as accurate as it is today, and this was the key to the case. If Phyllis had been killed between 11 p.m. and 11.30 p.m., Wood could easily have committed the murder. But if she had died between 3 a.m. and 5 p.m., as the police doctor testified, then the killer was an unknown 'customer' whom Phyllis had taken back to the house.

In 1909 Walter Sickert painted a picture called 'What shall we do for the rent?' showing a nude woman on a bed with a clothed man sitting besides her. It is believed that Sickert, who lived nearby in Mornington Crescent, was inspired to paint it by Phyllis's death, as he included it in a series of paintings which he called 'The Camden Town Murder'. In 2002 American crime writer Patricia

Camden Town murder. Image '2' shows one of most important witnesses, and number '1' shows Sir Charles Mathews (silk hat) who conducted the prosecution. Number 3 shows Robert Wood.

Cornwall used the paintings as part of her attempt to prove that Sickert was not only responsible for Phyllis' murder but was also Jack the Ripper. Her Ripper theory has not gained wide acceptance.

Some years after the case, Marshall Hall met a small man outside a court who said: 'I see you don't know me, Sir Edward'.

'No, I'm afraid I don't – please forgive me. I have a terrible memory for faces,' Marshall Hall replied. He looked at the man's deep sunk eyes and long artistic fingers and said: 'Why yes, isn't your name Wood – Robert Wood?'

'No,' replied the man as he turned away, 'it's not, but I'd like you to know I'm doing very well – and I owe it all to you.' Bob Wood married in 1915 and lived quietly at No. 13 Embankment Gardens in Chelsea from at least 1945 until his death in 1966.

AD 1910

CRIPPEN

The Quiet Man in Glasses

ONE OF THE reasons that this case is still remembered is the fascinating combination of an ordinary man and the brutality of the crime. In 1910, Dr Hawley Harvey Crippen was convicted of murdering his wife Cora at No. 39 Hilldrop Crescent, off the Camden Road, where remains of a torso were found buried in the cellar. Though it is a notorious London crime, both the doctor and his wife were in fact Americans.

Crippen was born in 1862 in Coldwater, Michigan, the son of a dry goods merchant. He studied for a medical degree and, later, a diploma in homeopathic medicine. He married Charlotte Bell, a student nurse, in 1887. They had a son, Otto, but five years later Charlotte died while pregnant with their second child. Crippen moved to Brooklyn, working as an assistant GP. There he fell in love with a patient, seventeen-year-old Cora Turner, the mistress of a wealthy stove manufacturer.

Cora was born as Kunigunde Mackamotzki on 3 September 1873. A vivacious personality, she had large dark eyes and raven black hair, a loud voice and a strong New York accent. She dressed in the brightest colours and her appearance was likened by a friend to a bird of paradise. In contrast, Crippen was short, slight in stature, with a sandy moustache, prominent eyes that stared out through gold-rimmed spectacles and a large domed forehead. They were married on 1 September 1892 in Jersey

Portrait of Crippen from 1910.

City. Crippen went to work for Munyon's Homoeopathic Remedy Co. and was sent to London in 1897, to manage the company's new branch in Shaftsbury Avenue. They lived nearby, at No. 34 Store Street.

Cora had adopted the name 'Belle Elmore' to pursue a career on the music-hall stage as a singer and comedienne, but never made it to the top of the bill. She played the Bedford in Camden Town on a number of occasions, and became the treasurer of the Music Hall Ladies' Guild which helped less fortunate members of the profession.

Belle put on weight and bullied her small, meek husband, who soon noted a change in his wife's feelings. 'She was always finding fault with me,' he later said, 'and every night she took some opportunity of quarrelling with me. She said she had met Bruce Miller (fellow American and music hall performer) and had got very fond of him, and did not care for me any more.'

But Crippen continued to support Belle's career and pay for furs, lavish gowns and expensive jewellery. Always courteous, polite and hospitable, friends said he was a good husband, a kind-hearted and amiable man.

In September 1905 the Crippens rented No. 39 Hilldrop Crescent, where they took in lodgers to help pay the bills. Crippen had to clean the boarders' boots, get the coal and lay the breakfast before leaving for work. He became a regular at his local pub, the Brecknock Arms, on most evenings. Crippen said he and Belle had stopped sleeping together, but by now Crippen was himself having an affair.

'Belle Elmore', better known as Cora Crippen. (LC-DIG-ggbain-05164)

In 1901 he had begun work at the Drouet Institute for the Deaf, opposite Primrose Hill, sending out mail order remedies (including plasters to stick behind the ear to cure deafness!). He became friendly with his young secretary, Ethel Le Neve. Ethel was a quiet, reserved young woman, the complete opposite of Belle. Born in Norfolk, she was then living with her parents over a butcher's shop at No. 61 Gayton Road, Hampstead. Their affair began in December 1904. Ethel moved into No. 80 Constantine Road near South End Green, Hampstead, in late 1908 and seems to have suffered a miscarriage a few weeks later. 'Hub and wifie', as Crippen and Edith called each other, had their secret love nest at No. 82 Wells Street, near Tottenham Court Road, where Crippen rented rooms under the name of 'Mr Franckel'.

On 31 January 1910 Crippen invited Clara and Paul Martinetti, fellow Americans and musical hall friends of Belle's, to supper at Hilldrop Crescent. This was the last time Belle was seen alive. At his trial, Crippen said he quarrelled with his wife after the guests left at 1.30 a.m. Belle said she was leaving him, and when he came home the following evening there was no sign of her. It is thought that Crippen had in fact poisoned her at breakfast and then gone to work as usual.

On 2 February, the Ladies' Guild held their regular weekly meeting. The secretary had two letters from Belle, openly written on her behalf by Crippen. In them she tendered her resignation, saying she'd been called to America at very short notice and didn't know when she'd be back. That same day, Ethel said Crippen had told her Belle had left him. A few weeks later guests were surprised to see Ethel wearing a distinctive diamond sunburst brooch of Belle's, and some of her furs, when she partnered Crippen at the Guild Ball. Edith finally moved in with Crippen at Hilldrop Crescent on 12 March. When he was asked about his wife, Crippen told her friends that she'd died of pneumonia on 23 March in America. On 26 March 1910 he published a brief death notice in *Era*, the theatre's trade paper.

SUSPICION GROWS

The members of the guild were very concerned about Belle. They even hired a private investigator – who discovered no trace of Belle on the transatlantic passenger lists. On 30 June John Nash and his wife, the popular music hall actress and guild member Lil Hawthorne, went to Scotland Yard and asked their friend Superintendent Frank Froest to investigate the disappearance of Mrs Crippen. They had just returned from America, where they had failed to find any trace of Belle.

At about 10 a.m. on 8 July, Chief Inspector Walter Dew and Sergeant Mitchell went to Hilldrop Crescent. There they met Ethel Le Neve, who seemed to be agitated. She took them to see Crippen in New Oxford Street, where he was running a dental business. Realising his story about Belle's disappearance was being questioned, Crippen made a confession: 'I suppose I had better tell the truth. The stories I have told about her death are untrue. As far as I know, she is still alive.' He believed she was in Chicago, he said, with her lover, Bruce Miller. The police took down a lengthy statement, even buying Crippen lunch in a local Italian restaurant. Then the four of them returned to Hilldrop Crescent, where Crippen invited the police to search the house.

Ethel was in tears after the police left at around 8 p.m. The couple spent a long time talking in their bedroom and, although no charge had been made against him, Crippen told Ethel there was nothing for it: they had to run away. Surely this was a drastic step for an innocent man to take? At his trial, Crippen said he believed that he'd be arrested if he couldn't produce Belle.

On Saturday 9 July, Crippen went to the office as normal. He asked his assistant William Long to go and buy some boy's clothes. But later, when Ethel put them on, she found that the trousers were too small and split. They laughed as Crippen crudely cut her hair: 'No one will recognise you. You are a perfect boy.' In her later account, Ethel said it was all part of the adventure. The couple took the night boat to Holland, moving on to Brussels, where they spent eight days. Crippen signed the hotel register as 'Mr John Robinson', and told the hotel that he was accompanied by his sixteen-year-old son.

When Chief Inspector Dew and Sergeant Mitchell revisited Hilldrop Crescent, they found that Crippen and Ethel had gone. A thorough search on Wednesday 13 July revealed human remains under the cellar floor; once the grave was opened, the smell of putrefaction was overpowering. The remains presented a truly bizarre spectacle: all of the bones, the limbs and the head were missing; these were never found, and the police speculated that Crippen may have disposed of them in the Regent's Canal.

An arrest warrant was issued and, after William Long had spoken to Dew, the couple's description was amended to read that Ethel could be disguised as a boy. 'The North London Cellar Murder' became front-page news. The police were criticised for letting the couple escape and investigated sightings from all over the country and Europe. Crippen booked a passage on the SS *Montrose*, sailing from Antwerp to Quebec on 20 July. Captain Henry Kendall had read their descriptions in the newspapers and, within hours of beginning the voyage, he became suspicious of the behaviour of 'Mr Robinson' and his sixteen-year-old son. His belief that he had

Crippen on board grew after he spoke to 'Mr Robinson' and noted his American accent and his medical knowledge about seasickness. On 22 July, he alerted the police using the ship's Marconi wireless telegram, a system which had only been in commercial use since 1907. Subsequently, Kendall received a £250 reward – but instead of cashing it, he had it framed.

Dew took a gamble and travelled undercover on the SS *Laurentic*, from Liverpool to Canada. Even though the *Montrose* had a three-day start, the *Laurentic*'s running time was four days shorter. While the chase was on, Captain Kendall sent regular radio reports to several English newspapers. Crippen and Ethel remained oblivious as the public back home followed the story with mounting interest. Later, Ethel said: 'It never entered my mind that any of the ship's officers had discovered my disguise.' Before the ship reached Quebec, Dew boarded the *Montrose* on 31 July, disguised as a pilot. On finding his quarry, the detective simply said, 'Good morning, Dr Crippen.' Crippen recognised Dew immediately and, to protect Ethel, quickly replied, 'It is only fair to say she knows nothing about it. I never told her anything.' At the trial the prosecution maintained that 'it' referred to Belle's murder.

Crippen and Ethel were arrested, extradited and returned to Liverpool, arriving there on 27 August. The next day Crippen and Ethel were secretly photographed in the Bow Street police court, where it was decided that Crippen would stand trial at the Old Bailey on 18 October 1910.

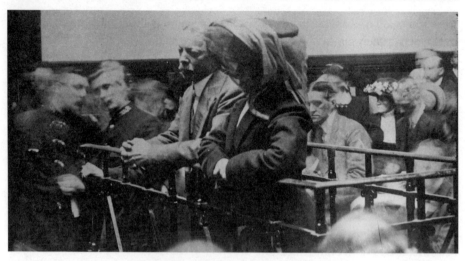

The famous – and illicit – photograph of Crippen and his mistress, Ethel Le Neve, in the dock. (LC-DIG-ggbain-08612)

THE EVIDENCE

At the trial the prosecution assembled several key pieces of evidence against Crippen:

- If Belle had gone to America, why had she left her jewellery and a large collection of clothes and furs behind?
- Belle had undergone an operation in America to remove her womb and ovaries, and was left with a distinctive scar. A piece of skin from the cellar showed an abdomen scar that corresponded to Belle's operation. Although the defence produced experts who said it was actually a skin fold, their evidence wasn't very convincing.
- Part of a pyjama jacket found buried with the remains had the maker's label 'Jones Brothers', a department store on the nearby Holloway Road. Store records revealed that on 5 January 1909 Belle had bought three sets of pyjamas of that particular fabric. (Today, Crippen's pyjama jacket is kept in the 'Black Museum' at Scotland Yard.)

- The poison hyoscine was found in the human remains at Hilldrop Crescent. Used as a sedative, it had never before – or since – been detected in a murder case. On 19 January Crippen had collected five grains of hyoscine hydrobromide from Lewis & Burrows, chemists, of No. 108 New Oxford Street, across the road from his office. He claimed he used it in his homeopathic remedies.

- Crippen's main line of defence was simple: the body in the cellar couldn't be Belle because she had gone to America to find her lover, Bruce Miller. But Miller was traced. Now a businessman of good standing in Chicago (and married with two children), his replies under cross-examination were guarded. He admitted to meeting Belle in London and sending her letters signed 'love and kisses to Brown Eyes', but said they'd never had an affair – and that she certainly hadn't contacted him in America.

After retiring for only twenty-seven minutes, the jury convicted Crippen of wilful murder. When asked if he had anything to say, Crippen said, 'I still protest my innocence.' Three judges denied Crippen's appeal and the Home Secretary, Winston Churchill, turned down a reprieve petition with 15,000 signatures. Crippen was hanged at Pentonville at 9 a.m. on the morning of 23 November 1910. When his waxwork went on display at Madame Tussauds it was said to be a perfect likeness. This is possibly explained by Tussaud family tradition which recalls that a small camera, concealed in a bowler hat, was used for the first time at Crippen's trial.

Walter Dew had a strange sort of respect for Crippen and called him 'a remarkable little man'. As a young policeman Dew had worked on the Ripper inquiry: 'compared with Jack the Ripper,' he said, 'Crippen was an angel.' Dew retired soon after the Crippen murder and died in Worthing, at the age of eighty-four, in 1947.

Belle's funeral at Finchley Cemetery on 11 October was arranged by the Ladies' Guild, and attended by a large crowd. On 25 October, four days after Crippen was sentenced to death, Ethel was tried as an accessory to the murder. The trial lasted a day, and after only twenty minutes the jury returned a 'not guilty' verdict. Ethel sold her life story, which was ghost-written and serialised in *Lloyd's Weekly News*. In 1913 she was living as Miss Harvey (Crippen's middle name) at Coalbrook Mansions,

in Balham, south London. Ethel married Stanley Smith in 1915. She moved to Croydon and had two children. She kept her name and connection to Crippen a secret from her family right up to her death in 1967. In his recent book *Supper with the Crippens*, David Smith argues that Ethel must have known what happened to Belle, and that she was very lucky to have been found innocent.

NO. 39 HILLDROP CRESCENT

After the trials and the huge publicity, No. 39 Hilldrop Crescent was bought by the Scottish music hall artist Sandy McNab. He turned it into a Crippen museum, but was forced to abandon the scheme after neighbours complained. The house was bombed on 8 September 1940 and later replaced by a block of flats, 'Margaret Bondfield House', named after the first British woman MP to become a cabinet minister (in 1929).

100 YEARS LATER

In a recent twist to the Crippen story, research at Michigan State University (2007) claimed that DNA from the cellar remains did not match those of Cora's relatives. The DNA also seemed to be a male, rather than female. This has raised new questions about who was buried under the floor – and, by implication, about Crippen's guilt. But the findings have since been challenged on both the accuracy of the genealogy and the DNA technique used.

WARTIME CAMDEN

LIKE MANY PARTS of London, Camden suffered from air attacks during the First World War. The first raid happened on 8 September 1915 when bombs from a Zeppelin airship fell on Holborn. One man was killed and sixteen wounded in Theobalds Road; the blast broke the gas main in Lambs Conduit Passage and damaged a block of buildings (including the Dolphin pub, which caught fire). The old clock, which was recovered after the attack, is on display in the pub today, and shows that the hands stopped at 10.40 p.m. – the exact time that the bar was demolished. Three men died at the pub. The bomb was dropped by Zeppelin L13, under the command of Zeppelin 'ace' Heinrich Mathy. A year later, on 1 October 1916, Mathy died when his Zeppelin was shot down over Potters Bar by Lt Wulstan Joseph Tempest of 39 Squadron. The remains of Mathy and his crew were buried in a local cemetery, but in the 1960s they were moved to the German Military Cemetery at Cannock Chase. Mathy was the most successful Zeppelin commander, taking part in fifteen raids over England.

On the night of 13 October 1915, the Revd Phillip Sidney, a curate at St Alban's, Holborn, came close to death when he returned to his rooms in Gray's Inn Square:

I heard a terrific explosion nearby. 'The Zeppelins are here again,' I said to myself. 'I'm going to get out of this, downstairs is safer.' I got as far as the landing. At that moment the next bomb exploded in the garden just beneath my rooms. All I remember is the loudest explosion I ever heard accompanied by a loud incessant singing noise in my ears. Then I saw a great oak door suddenly lift itself off its hinges and fly past me at great speed, just missing my head. There was a noise of falling brickwork and flying glass all around me. A terrific tornado of wind took me off my feet and I found myself flying through the air and then everything seemed suddenly to go out – complete blank and darkness. The next thing I remember was a bright light shining in my eyes and two tall people standing over me talking to one another. I heard one say, 'He's dead, I'm afraid to get him out of this.' I woke up with a start and said, 'No, I'm not. I have been blown up by a Zepp. Bomb.'

Odhams Printing Works, just over the Camden boundary in Long Acre, were destroyed by an incendiary bomb on 28 January 1918, with great loss of life.

Phillip had been blown down two flights of stairs and into the street, where he lay buried under brickwork. Amazingly, his only injuries were minor bruises and aches.

At first, the Zeppelin raids brought people out on the streets to watch them rather than take cover. Subsequent raids were made by Gotha and the huge Staaken Giant aircraft rather than airships.

On 7 July 1917 a man was killed and three more injured in St Pancras Road when the nearby Midland Railway goods station was severely damaged. A bomb landed opposite the Bedford Hotel in Southampton Row on 24 September 1917 and there were heavy casualties; thirteen people died and twenty-six were injured. The worst raid was on 17 February 1918 when five bombs killed twenty people and injured twenty-two at St Pancras station. Edith Gooday was sheltering with her family below the Midland Hotel at St Pancras:

There was a terrific crash and darkness descended. Showers of splintering glass fell around us and coal dust fell, it seemed, by the ton. Those of us who were not lying on the ground bleeding and groaning were practically choking... Suddenly a ray of light descended and framed in the doorway was a man in uniform. He told us the raid had been over for some time. So we tried to leave, all this time we had been in a corner behind a pillar. When we moved, we seemed to be ankle-deep in broken glass, and as we left the ruins, matches flickered and in their light a ghastly sight met our eyes: dead and injured lay everywhere. Picking our way carefully, we at last came out into the air to see in the distance flames leaping up to the sky.

Warnings of Zeppelin raids used to the recruiters' benefit. (LC-USZC4-10972)

Lena Ford, who wrote the hugely popular wartime song, 'Keep the Home Fires Burning', was killed in one of the last raids of the war on 7 March, just over the Camden boundary in Maida Vale.

THE SECOND WORLD WAR

After the so-called 'phoney war', air raids on London began on 7 September 1940. The following nights there were attacks on St Pancras and Hampstead. During the Blitz, which lasted from September 1940 until May 1941, thousands of high explosive, incendiary, parachute and other types of bombs hit the borough.

People again sought shelter in underground stations. The 'Air Raid Shelterers' at Swiss Cottage started a magazine (called, appropriately enough, *The Swiss Cottager*). It urged people not to reserve places or use deck chairs as they took up too much space, and to take their litter with them each morning. Local authorities eventually fitted stations with bunk beds and toilets and provided refreshments. Many householders were given Anderson shelters to erect in their back gardens or indoor Morrison shelters, which saved many lives. Deep shelters were built below eight underground stations, three of them in Camden: Belsize Park, Camden Town and Goodge Street. They are still in use today, as secure storage for commercial archives. The Belsize Park shelter has over 5,000ft of tunnels, running from the corner of Upper Park Road to a point under the Royal Free Hospital.

London was attacked by 685 bombers on the night of 16/17 April 1941. This was the worst raid on Holborn when more than 100 people died and over 400 buildings were severely damaged or destroyed. St Alban's church, where the Revd Sidney had previously been curate, was gutted. A parachute mine wrecked several blocks of flats, killing forty-seven people in Portpool Lane, and twenty Canadian servicemen died when their temporary hostel in Malet Street was hit by a huge bomb. The heavy raid on

SECOND WORLD WAR DEATHS AND SERIOUS INJURIES ACROSS THE BOROUGH OF CAMDEN

	Deaths	Serious Injuries
Borough of Hampstead	204	930
Borough of St Pancras	957	1,443
Borough of Holborn	426	621
Total	1,587	2,994

These figures compare with almost 30,000 deaths and 50,500 injuries across the whole of the London region.

10/11 May resulted in fewer casualties. Incendiary bombs hit the King's Library at the British Library and more than 1,000 rare and priceless books were damaged, while the famous Holborn Empire was badly damaged and never re-opened.

A terrible family tragedy occurred on 19 February 1944 when a party was being held in a flat over 263 West End Lane. Harry Elcome was a soldier who was going to be married later that day. At 1.10 a.m. a high-explosive bomb demolished the upper part of the building, and a fire broke out. Rescue services tried to work their way up from the basement but were constantly beaten back by the flames and falling debris. Tragically, the only survivor of the family party of eleven men, women and young children was Harry's father, painter and decorator Thomas Elcome. Two of the children were aged just four months and six months.

Towards the end of the war the Germans used their 'vengeance weapons', the V1 'doodlebug' and the V2 long-range rocket. Beginning in June 1944, twenty 'Flying Bombs' or V1s landed in Hampstead; twenty hit St Pancras and four exploded in Holborn. People hated the roaring noise of the V1s which was described as 'a sort of stuttering, rattling, deep-throated growl', but vastly preferred the sound to the silence that followed when the engine cut out. It then fell out of the sky, exploding when it hit the ground: 'There was something quite eerie about these monsters with nobody in them.' On 29 June 1944 a V1 fell on Mortimer Crescent in Kilburn, wrecking many houses and forcing the writer George

A moment of joy amidst the ruins: a dog and her pups rescued in Weedington Road, Kentish Town, in 1941. (Courtesy of Camden Local Studies and Archive Centre)

Orwell, who was renting the basement of No. 10, to move to Islington.

The V2s arrived without warning and caused massive damage. Three hit Hampstead, while three landed in St Pancras, and two exploded in Holborn. In one of the last air raids of the war a V2 rocket fell on Smithfield Market soon after 11 a.m. on 8 March 1945. It penetrated to the railway lines below and exploded, demolishing buildings that fell into a huge crater. Earlier that morning, Leonard Lincoln had collected £1,250,000 from the Bank of England and, having delivered it to his bank in the city, was passing the market. His van was only 25 yards

---

A CURIOUS INCIDENT DURING THE SECOND WORLD WAR

Bridget Jennings was crossing Hampstead Heath, on her way to work, when she spotted an envelope marked 'TOP SECRET'. She handed it over to her boss at Naval Intelligence. The envelope had been dropped the previous evening, and contained a draft of 'Operation Torch', the British-American invasion of North Africa in 1942. Winston Churchill reportedly bit through his cigar when he was told! The careless culprit had no right to be carrying the envelope; he was later court martialled and dismissed from the RAF. In June 1944 Bridget was awarded the British Empire Medal for her prompt action in preventing what might have been a disaster for the Allied Forces.

---

from the point of impact when the engine burst into flames. He escaped but had to be rescued after he fell into the crater. Market worker Ron Fowler was enveloped in a thick black fog of dust and dirt. Stumbling to escape, he realized, to his horror, he was standing on something soft: a dead body, lying face down in the rubble. Buildings within a 0.25-mile radius were rendered unsafe, and every structure on twenty-nine adjoining streets was damaged. A total of 110 people died; 123 were seriously injured, and 243 received lesser injuries. Contemporary reports say the market was particularly crowded that morning because a consignment of rabbits or fish was on sale, a rare treat for Londoners used to strict rationing.

AD 1955

THE BLONDE AND THE PLAYBOY

Ruth Ellis and David Blakely

ON 10 APRIL 1955, the Magdala pub in South End Park, Hampstead, was the scene of a shooting that sent Ruth Ellis to the gallows. The last woman to be hanged in Britain, the outcry that followed Ruth's execution was instrumental in bringing about significant changes to the law.

Ruth was born in North Wales in 1926. Her father, Arthur Hornby, changed the family name to 'Neilson', the name which appears on Ruth's birth certificate. Unable to get regular employment as a musician, Arthur became increasingly violent and abused both Ruth and her sister Muriel. The family moved to war-time London in 1941, where fifteen-year-old Ruth got waitressing and factory work. She moved on to acting lessons and to singing in a band. But when she became pregnant by a French-Canadian soldier, Ruth discovered that her lover had a wife back home, meaning that they couldn't marry. The baby, Clare Andre (Andy) McCallum, was born in 1944 and brought up by Muriel and by Ruth's mother.

Ruth started working for Morris Conley, who has been described as 'being in the centre of corruption in the West End of London'. After the war, he bought up properties and let flats to girls who worked as hostesses in his clubs. There Ruth met George Ellis, known on the circuit as 'the mad dentist'. That alone should have rung alarm bells, for George was indeed a dentist but also an abusive alcoholic. He was forty-one. Ruth was just twenty-four. They married in 1950, and moved to Southampton. Their daughter Georgina was born the following year, after the couple had split up and Ruth had returned to London. Morris promptly made her the manageress of his 'Little Club' at No. 27

The Magdala pub.

Brompton Road, throwing in a free flat over the premises into the bargain.

In August 1953 an admirer of Ruth's, Desmond Cussen, introduced her to the good-looking twenty-four-year-old David Blakely. Blakely's background was very different to Ruth's: a comfortable middle-class family, with parents who financially supported him. David shared his step-father's passion for racing cars, but otherwise he wasn't keen on working. He tried, unsuccessfully, to develop a sports car with friend Ant (Anthony) Findlater while enjoying an affair with Ant's wife Carole.

Ruth and David were living together inside a fortnight. Marriage was promised but unlikely to happen. David knew his parents wouldn't approve of Ruth, her background or her job, and she terminated a pregnancy early in 1954. Morris Conley, meanwhile, disliked David, who caused scenes at the Little Club. On one occasion he hit Ruth across the face. Takings fell from around £200 a week to under £80. Ruth left – possibly fired by Conley – and went to live with Desmond Cussen in his flat, No. 20 Goodwood Court, Devonshire Street. They'd had a brief affair but Ruth rejected his offer of marriage and continued to see Blakely.

David and Ruth's relationship continued on its downward spiral, increasingly unstable and violent. By New Year of 1955, both had told friends that they wanted to separate. At the same time, they were intensely jealous of one another. Ruth moved out of Cussen's flat and he loaned her cash to rent a room at No. 44 Egerton Gardens, Kensington, where she lived with David. That March Ruth was again pregnant, but this time she miscarried, following a violent row with Blakely.

As Easter approached, Ruth was beginning to feel more hopeful about the future; 'David was quite happy,' she later said, 'and he was saying everything would be alright, talking about marriage again.'

On 8 April, Good Friday, she believed they parted on the very best of terms. Blakely went to Hampstead to see Ant Findlater at his flat at No. 29 Tanza Road. But when he didn't come home, Ruth got Desmond to drive her to Hampstead. There she saw David's car – and suddenly filled with jealousy, she smashed three of the windows. Always jealous of Carole, Ruth now feared the Findlaters were using their au pair to lure David away. All Saturday Ruth hung around Tanza Road. Then, returning to Egerton Gardens, she spent a second sleepless night and drinking heavily.

On the evening of 10 April, Easter Sunday, the Findlaters threw a party. When they ran out of cigarettes and beer, David and a fellow guest drove to the nearby Magdala public house to buy supplies. But Ruth had again come looking for David, and was seen peering in at the pub window. When the men left the Magdala, Ruth called out 'David!' – and then she shot him. She fired six times as he tried to escape. Four bullets entered his body, one into his back from just 3in away, as he lay on the pavement. Ruth was quite calm afterwards, and surrendered to an off-duty policeman. David was pronounced dead upon his arrival at New End Hospital.

Ruth Ellis's trial at the Old Bailey began on 20 June and was one of the shortest murder trials on record,

The bullet holes which can still be seen in the wall of the Magdala pub.

ending the following day. She appeared confident, was dressed smartly and had been allowed to peroxide dye her hair. Sadly, this last wasn't the smartest move: someone in the public gallery loudly exclaimed, 'Blonde tart!' You needed a ticket to attend and, outside, they were exchanging hands for £30 – over £600 today.

Ruth pleaded 'not guilty'. The prosecution repeated her statement to the police: 'When I put the gun in my bag I intended to find David and shoot him.' Society's prejudices were ranged against her: a divorcee with two children by different fathers, who had affairs with two men at once and earned her living working in a club. At the time there were only four available defences against a murder charge: the accused didn't do it; was insane; or acted in self-defence; finally, if sufficient provocation existed, the charge could be reduced to manslaughter. This was the only one available to Ruth's QC. Although Ruth did not make a good witness – 'she did nothing to counter the view that she was a cold-hearted "tart" who had shot her lover' – it has since been argued that her defence was poorly handled. Her QC failed to draw out how damaged she was, and how desperate she'd been, when she shot Blakely. Ruth's cross-examination by the prosecution consisted of a single question: what had she intended to do when she fired the revolver at close range into David Blakely's body? Ruth replied: 'It is obvious that when I shot him I intended to kill him.'

The judge ruled that the charge could not be reduced to manslaughter, and concluded: 'even if you accept every word of Mrs Ellis's evidence there does not seem to be anything in it which establishes any sort of defence to the charge of murder.' The jury took twenty-three minutes to return their verdict of 'guilty', with no recommendation to mercy. Ruth was returned to Holloway Prison to await her execution on 13 July. Many were outraged at the verdict and campaigned for a reprieve. Ruth herself appeared resigned to death, saying she wanted to join Blakely, but she eventually agreed to ask for clemency. American author Raymond Chandler wrote, 'it was a crime of passion committed, I feel certain, under a kind of shock which may have flared up uncontrollably.' But there were letters supporting the verdict, including an influential one from Mrs Gladys Kensington Yule, a banker's wife injured by a ricocheting bullet outside the Magdala: 'Don't let us turn Ruth Ellis into a national hero. I stood petrified and watched her kill David Blakely in cold blood. As it is, I have a partly crippled right hand for life.'

The Home Secretary refused a reprieve. On the 12th, Ruth made a desperate confession to her lawyer, stating that on the 10th she and Cussen had been drinking heavily – and that he had given her the loaded gun and driven her to Hampstead. Her friend Jackie Dyer had already made a statement to this effect. But there was to be no last-minute pardon. Ruth was hanged the following morning at 9 a.m. at Holloway Prison, and buried inside prison grounds. The Pathé News website (http://www.britishpathe.com) shows the crowds waiting outside the prison. And as happened to so many murderers before her, Ruth's waxwork went on display in Blackpool inside twenty-four hours.

THE AFTERMATH

Ruth's execution was instrumental in bringing about the 1957 Homicide Act, which included the concept of diminished responsibility, and, in 1969, the abolition of the death penalty.

Ruth's body was exhumed on 31 March 1971 and reinterred at St Mary's church, Amersham, with a simple memorial: 'Ruth Hornby, 1926-1955'. David Blakely lies nearby at Penn. His tombstone reads: 'He was of great heart, courtly and courageous.'

In 1972 John Bickford, one of Ruth's lawyers, made a statement to the police.

He said Desmond Cussen had admitted to him that he'd given the gun to Ruth and showed her how to fire it. Cussen emigrated to Australia in 1964. When questioned by a reporter in 1977, he denied any involvement – including Ruth's statement. He died in 1991.

In August 1958 Ruth's former husband George Ellis was found dead in a hotel room in Jersey. He'd killed himself using the cord of his pyjama trousers. Their daughter Georgina had by that point been adopted. She wrote *A Murder of Passion* in 1995, telling Ruth's story and showing how her own life mirrored her mother's in several respects. Georgina died in 2001. Ruth's son Andy was found dead in 1982, at Sale Place, Paddington, two weeks after taking an overdose of sleeping pills. His ashes were interred in his mother's grave.

Ruth's sister Muriel Jakubait (with Monica Weller) wrote *Ruth Ellis: My Sister's Secret Life* (2005), a book which includes links to the Secret Service and to Dr Stephen Ward (of the Profumo scandal). In it, she claims that Cussen, not Ruth, fired the fatal shot. In 2003 Muriel's appeal for Ruth's conviction to be overturned was denied.

David Blakely was the victim of a brutal shooting, but today it is unlikely that Ruth Ellis would have been found guilty of his murder.